TRANSPORTATION ISSUES, POLICIES AND R&D

PERFORMANCE-BASED TRANSPORTATION PROGRAMS

ASSESSMENTS OF APPROACHES AND CHALLENGES

TRANSPORTATION ISSUES, POLICIES AND R&D

Additional books in this series can be found on Nova's website under the Series tab.

Additional e-books in this series can be found on Nova's website under the e-book tab.

TRANSPORTATION ISSUES, POLICIES AND R&D

PERFORMANCE-BASED TRANSPORTATION PROGRAMS

ASSESSMENTS OF APPROACHES AND CHALLENGES

TRAVIS SCHMIDT
EDITOR

nova publishers
New York

NOTICE TO THE READER

Library of Congress Cataloging-in-Publication Data

ISBN: 978-1-63482-722-5

Published by Nova Science Publishers, Inc. † New York

CONTENTS

PREFACE

This book examines the progress that DOT has made in developing a national performance-based approach to surface transportation; and the challenges states and other grantees report facing in implementing this approach. This book also reports on the extent to which federal transit programs use performance information in making decisions about funding distribution and in evaluating the programs' effectiveness; mechanisms for making these programs more performance based, and strategies for supporting their successful implementation; and how selected U.S. and foreign transit agencies have used performance measurement in their planning and decisions, and their views on the federal role in transit.

Chapter 1 – In fiscal year 2013, DOT provided about $50 billion to states and other grantees (such as metropolitan planning organizations and transit agencies) to support highway and transit infrastructure and safety. However, it is not clear if this funding has improved system performance because, in part, these programs have lacked links to performance and national goals. Since 2008, GAO has highlighted the need to link surface transportation programs to performance. MAP-21 transformed surface transportation programs by including provisions for both DOT and its grantees to move toward a national performance-based approach, in many cases holding grantees accountable for performance for the first time. This approach includes DOT establishing national performance measures, and states and other grantees setting targets related to these measures, and reporting progress.

GAO examined (1) the progress that DOT has made in developing a national performance-based approach to surface transportation and (2) the challenges states and other grantees report facing in implementing this approach. GAO reviewed proposed rules and DOT information on rulemaking milestones and interviewed officials from DOT, national transportation organizations, and a non-generalizable sample of 29 grantees in 13 states, selected on the basis of state population growth, performance management experience, and other factors. DOT reviewed a draft of this report and provided technical comments, which were incorporated as appropriate.

Chapter 2 – Public demand and federal funding for transit have grown in recent years, yet most of this funding is not tied to performance. As Congress prepares for reauthorization of the federal surface transportation programs, GAO was asked to report on (1) the extent to which federal transit programs use performance information in making decisions about funding distribution and in evaluating the programs' effectiveness; (2) mechanisms for making these programs more performance based, and strategies for supporting their successful implementation; and (3) how selected U.S. and foreign transit agencies have used performance measurement in their planning and decisions, and their views on the federal role in transit. To do so, GAO analyzed legislation, federal documents, and literature; interviewed federal officials and transit experts; and conducted semistructured interviews with selected transit agencies using criteria that, for U.S. agencies, covered a variety of regions and population sizes and, for foreign agencies, multiple transit modes and English language capability.

Chapter 3 – Through the statewide transportation planning process, states decide how to spend federal transportation funds—almost $46 billion in fiscal year 2009. Draft legislation to reauthorize federal surface transportation legislation would, among other things, revise planning requirements to recognize states' use of rural planning organizations (RPO) and require performance measurement. As requested, GAO examined (1) states' planning activities and RPOs' satisfaction that rural needs are considered, (2) states' planning challenges, (3) the U.S. Department of Transportation's (USDOT) approach to overseeing statewide planning, and (4) states' use of performance measurement and opportunities to make statewide planning more performance based. GAO analyzed planning documents; surveyed departments of transportation in 50 states, Puerto Rico, and Washington, D.C., and 569 RPOs; interviewed officials in 6 states; and held an expert panel on performance-based planning.

In: Performance-Based Transportation Programs ISBN: 978-1-63482-722-5
Editor: Travis Schmidt

Chapter 1

SURFACE TRANSPORTATION: DOT IS PROGRESSING TOWARD A PERFORMANCE-BASED APPROACH, BUT STATES AND GRANTEES REPORT POTENTIAL IMPLEMENTATION CHALLENGES*

United States Government Accountability Office

ABBREVIATIONS

AASHTO	American Association of State Highway and Transportation Officials
ANPRM	Advance Notice of Proposed Rulemaking
AMPO	Association of Metropolitan Planning Organizations
APA	Administrative Procedures Act
DOT	Department of Transportation
FHWA	Federal Highway Administration
FMCSA	Federal Motor Carrier Safety Administration
FTA	Federal Transit Administration
GHSA	Governors Highway Safety Association
MAP-21	Moving Ahead for Progress in the 21st Century Act

* This is an edited, reformatted and augmented version of The United States Government Accountability Office publication, GAO-15-217, dated January 2015.

MPO	metropolitan planning organization
NARC	National Association of Regional Councils
NHTSA	National Highway Traffic Safety Administration
OMB	Office of Management and Budget
STIP	state transportation improvement program
TIP	transportation improvement program

Why GAO Did This Study

In fiscal year 2013, DOT provided about $50 billion to states and other grantees (such as metropolitan planning organizations and transit agencies) to support highway and transit infrastructure and safety. However, it is not clear if this funding has improved system performance because, in part, these programs have lacked links to performance and national goals. Since 2008, GAO has highlighted the need to link surface transportation programs to performance. MAP-21 transformed surface transportation programs by including provisions for both DOT and its grantees to move toward a national performance-based approach, in many cases holding grantees accountable for performance for the first time. This approach includes DOT establishing national performance measures, and states and other grantees setting targets related to these measures, and reporting progress.

GAO examined (1) the progress that DOT has made in developing a national performance-based approach to surface transportation and (2) the challenges states and other grantees report facing in implementing this approach. GAO reviewed proposed rules and DOT information on rulemaking milestones and interviewed officials from DOT, national transportation organizations, and a non-generalizable sample of 29 grantees in 13 states, selected on the basis of state population growth, performance management experience, and other factors. DOT reviewed a draft of this report and provided technical comments, which were incorporated as appropriate.

What GAO Found

The Department of Transportation (DOT) has made progress moving toward a national performance-based approach since the Moving Ahead for Progress in the 21st Century Act (MAP-21) was enacted in July 2012. DOT has undertaken extensive outreach efforts with states and other grantees and is developing nine rules that, among other things, are to establish national performance measures, and target-setting and reporting requirements for grantees. Five of the rules have been released for public comment, and none has been finalized. DOT has missed five of six deadlines established by MAP-21. However, given the extent to which MAP-21 transformed surface transportation programs and the length and complexity of the rulemaking process, these deadlines may have been ambitious. DOT's progress has also been affected by the varying experiences within its operating administrations in implementing a performance-based approach. For example, the National Highway Traffic Safety Administration has been implementing such an approach in its grant programs since 2008, while other DOT operating administrations started more recently.

States and other grantees reported potential data and cost challenges with implementing a national performance-based approach. According to some grantees and national organizations GAO contacted, data may not be available for measuring performance in some areas, such as congestion, and collecting data that are available may prove difficult. For example, DOT has proposed states collect traffic data on all public roads, and some state officials told GAO this step would be a substantial undertaking; New York officials told GAO that the state has adequate data for only about 37 percent of its public roads. Further, some grantees noted they may lack the staff or resources to analyze data, and some raised concerns that implementation costs may be substantial. DOT officials acknowledged these challenges and are working with grantees to help overcome obstacles. For example, DOT is working with states to share data, best practices, and templates for reporting.

* * *

January 16, 2015

The Honorable Bill Shuster
Chairman
Committee on Transportation and Infrastructure
House of Representatives

The Honorable Peter DeFazio
House of Representatives

The U.S. Department of Transportation (DOT) annually provides billions of dollars to states and other grantees to improve the nation's highway and transit infrastructure and safety. DOT provides federal funding to these grantees, including states, transit agencies, and metropolitan planning organizations[1] (MPO), primarily through programs administered by three of its operating administrations: The Federal Highway Administration (FHWA), which administers the federal-aid highway program that provides billions to states for highway and bridge projects; the National Highway Traffic Safety Administration (NHTSA), which provides grant funding to support state highway safety programs; and the Federal Transit Administration (FTA), which administers a variety of grant programs that provide funding for the development and expansion of bus, rail and other transit projects, among other things. In fiscal year 2013, DOT provided approximately $50 billion to grantees for surface transportation projects through the programs administered by FHWA, FTA, and NHTSA.

However, it is not clear whether the federal funding provided to states and other grantees through these surface transportation programs has improved the Nation's system performance because, among other things, these programs have lacked links to performance and national goals. Since 2008, we have highlighted the need to link surface transportation programs to performance and target surface transportation resources more effectively.[2] In particular, we have noted that tracking specific outcomes that are clearly linked to program goals could provide a strong foundation for holding grant recipients responsible for achieving federal objectives and measuring program performance. Accordingly, we recommended that Congress consider reexamining and refocusing surface transportation programs to, among other things, make grantees more accountable through the use of more performance-based links between funding and program outcomes. Funding the nation's surface transportation system is on GAO's High Risk List. [3]

In July 2012, the President signed into law the Moving Ahead for Progress in the 21st Century Act (MAP-21) that included provisions for both DOT and its grantees to move toward a national performance-based approach for surface transportation.[4] Among other things, the act amended the United States Code to establish national surface transportation performance goals, and to provide a three-stage process for a national performance-based approach for surface transportation through which (1) DOT defines performance measures in support of the national goals and develops an approach for measuring grantee performance; (2) states and other grantees set and maintain targets based on the DOT-defined performance measures, collect data, and report to DOT their progress in meeting their targets; and (3) DOT evaluates grantee performance and reports to Congress on the extent to which grantees have met their targets. If progress toward meeting some targets is insufficient, states must report action they will undertake to achieve their targets. In addition, MAP-21 links funding to performance by requiring states to take corrective action if progress toward certain targets is insufficient, and to spend a specified portion of their annual federal funding to improve National Highway System[5] bridges and Interstate-system pavement should conditions fall below minimum standards set by MAP-21 and the Secretary of Transportation, respectively.[6] MAP-21 was originally enacted as a 2-year authorization for surface transportation programs through September 30, 2014. In August 2014, legislation was enacted that extended programs and funding authorized under MAP-21 until May 31, 2015.[7]

This report examines (1) the progress that DOT has made in developing a national performance-based approach to surface transportation and (2) the challenges states and other grantees report facing in implementing this approach. We prepared this report under the authority of the U.S. Comptroller General to conduct evaluations in light of broad congressional interest in this area and the relationship of this topic to our High-Risk area on funding the nation's surface transportation system.

To address these objectives, we reviewed academic literature from 2011 through 2014—representing the time period just before and since MAP-21 was enacted—as well as our body of work on performance management in the federal government and transportation programs. To describe the progress that DOT has made in developing a national performance-based approach for surface transportation programs, we reviewed related requirements and timetables in MAP-21 for FHWA, FTA, and NHTSA as well as interim and proposed rulemakings developed by these operating administrations in response to these requirements.[8] We did not evaluate the potential effectiveness of the proposed rules because the content may change before rules are finalized in response to comments submitted by grantees and other parties. We also analyzed DOT documents, guidance, and other information provided to grantees and analyzed DOT information on estimated and completed rulemaking milestones to understand the progress FHWA, FTA, and NHTSA have made developing the performance-based approach. We interviewed FHWA, FTA, and NHTSA officials to understand the factors affecting DOT's progress in developing the performance-based approach.

To understand the challenges states and other grantees face in implementing a performance-based approach to surface transportation, we analyzed comments submitted to DOT by—and interviewed officials from—national transportation organizations and 29 grantees in 13 states. The grantees comprised a sample of state transportation agencies, state highway safety offices, metropolitan and rural planning organizations, and transit agencies, selected to include grantees in states with varying population growth trends, population size, geographic location, transit infrastructure age, experiences managing and measuring transportation project performance, and incorporating recommendations from DOT and national transportation organizations. Based on these criteria, in four states, we interviewed officials from the state department of transportation, one or more metropolitan planning organizations, local transit providers, and DOT regional oversight offices;[9] in the remaining nine states, we interviewed officials from at least one state transportation agency, planning organization or transit agency in that state. The information gathered from these 29 grantees cannot be generalized to all federal surface transportation grantees; however, they provided insight into the types of challenges that some grantees anticipate in implementing DOT's future rulemaking and overall performance based approach, as well as, perspectives on DOT's outreach and rulemaking progress. Additional information on our scope and methodology can be found in appendix I.

We conducted this performance audit from May 2014 to January 2015 in accordance with generally accepted government auditing standards.

Those standards require that we plan and perform the audit to obtain sufficient, appropriate evidence to provide a reasonable basis for our findings and conclusions based on our audit objectives. We believe that the evidence obtained provides a reasonable basis for our findings and conclusions based on our audit objectives.

BACKGROUND

Most of the federal funding for highway and transit infrastructure and safety improvements is provided by FHWA, FTA, and NHTSA.

- FHWA provides about $38 billion each year, or nearly 93 percent of its overall budget, to states to design, construct and maintain the nation's roadway and bridge infrastructure through the federal-aid highway program.[10] These funds are distributed through annual apportionments established by statutory formulas. FHWA oversees the federal-aid highway program, primarily through its 52 division offices located in each state, the District of Columbia, and Puerto Rico. FHWA division offices have 10 to 61 staff each, depending on the size of the state's highway program and other factors. As of October 2014, FHWA had approximately 2,900 staff—about two-thirds in the field and the remaining third at FHWA headquarters in Washington, D.C.[11]

- FTA provides approximately $10.5 billion each year for transit project grants to states, transit agencies, and MPOs. The grant funding provided by FTA represents 98 percent of its overall $10.7 billion budget; the remaining portion of the budget funds the administration and oversight of its various grant programs by about 500 federal employees in its Washington, D.C., headquarters and 10 regional offices.
- NHTSA provides about $500 million per year, or about 60 percent of its annual budget of approximately $800 million, to state highway safety offices through grants. NHTSA awards these grants to state highway safety offices to support projects that focus on mitigating behavioral factors associated with crashes and improving traffic safety information systems, among other things. The remaining third of NHTSA's budget supports various highway and vehicle safety research and enforcement programs. NHTSA employs about 600 employees in its Washington, D.C. headquarters; its 10 regional offices; and its Vehicle Research and Test Center.

States develop a variety of plans as part of their overall transportation programs. Each state, as well as the District of Columbia and Puerto Rico, is required by statute to carry out a continuing, cooperative, and comprehensive statewide transportation planning process that requires periodic updates of plans.[12] The statewide transportation planning process addresses both urbanized and nonmetropolitan areas of the state and includes both highway and transit needs. As part of the statewide planning process, states must develop a long-range statewide transportation plan and a state transportation improvement program (STIP). The long-range statewide transportation plan establishes a state's strategic vision and direction for its transportation investments for at least a 20-year period. The STIP is the state program of transportation projects covering at least a 4-year period that are to be supported with federal surface transportation funds, as well as regionally significant projects requiring an action by FHWA or FTA, whether or not the projects are federally funded. At least every 4 years, state DOTs are required by statute to submit an updated STIP to FHWA and FTA for review and approval, in which the state certifies that the transportation planning process has been carried out in accordance with federal planning requirements.[13] In urbanized areas, MPOs are also required to produce a long-range transportation plan, referred to as a metropolitan transportation plan, and a transportation improvement program (TIP). We have previously found that the cycle and frequency of updates of these plans vary across states and MPOs.[14] In addition, each state is required to develop a strategic highway safety plan to, among other things, provide for performance management and identify strategies that cover all aspects of highway safety, which include (1) infrastructure improvements; (2) behavioral approaches, such as education and enforcement efforts meant to change drivers' behavior; and (3) emergency medical services. Furthermore, each year each state is required to develop a highway safety plan, describing the state's highway safety program and the activities they plan to undertake. According to NHTSA, states have voluntarily included measurable goals and objectives in their highway safety plans since 2010, enabling states to track the status of highway safety implementation efforts and monitor progress.

Prior to enactment of MAP-21 in 2012, DOT's surface transportation funding programs and statewide planning generally were not linked to performance-based outcomes, although some states used performance measures, most notably in the safety area. Historically, most federal surface transportation funds have been distributed through formulas that have only an indirect relationship to infrastructure needs, and many have no relationship to outcomes or grantees' performance.[15] FTA had incorporated performance-based principles into some of its formula grant programs to allocate funding. We previously found that about 5 percent of fiscal year 2010 funding for six formula grant programs we reviewed, on average, was required to be awarded based on transit agency performance.[16] In a 2010 report, we noted that DOT's oversight of the statewide planning process focused on state DOTs' compliance with planning process requirements and did not consider transportation planning outcomes.[17] At the state level, we found that states and MPOs have incorporated some performance measures and targets into their plans, though the use of measures and targets varied depending on the area. For example, we found nearly all state DOTs had safety performance measures and quantifiable targets related to these measures, due, in part, to the federal requirement that state DOTs develop a strategic highway safety plan that establishes statewide goals and objectives to reduce highway fatalities and serious injuries. In other areas, such as measuring truck freight traffic, vehicle congestion, and emissions, we noted states generally did not incorporate performance measures into their plans. However, even in areas such as safety where states had used performance measures, we reported that only a few states made significant attempts to integrate performance measurement into their statewide planning process to inform investment decisions.[18]

Since 2008, we have recommended that Congress consider reexamining and refocusing surface transportation programs to include performance-based principles.[19] In particular, we have noted that tracking specific outcomes that are clearly linked to program goals could provide a strong foundation for holding grant recipients responsible for achieving federal objectives and measuring overall program performance.[20] Furthermore, we have previously found that data-driven decision-making leads to better results, and that if agencies do not use performance measures and performance information to track progress to track progress toward goals, they may be at risk of failing to achieve their goals.[21] In addition, we found through our prior work that performance information can be used across a range of management functions to improve results, from setting program priorities and allocating resources to taking corrective action to solve program problems.

MAP-21 included a number of statutory requirements related to transforming the surface transportation system to a performance-based approach, for the operating administrations, as well as for states and other grantees, in many cases holding grantees accountable for the first time. For instance, MAP-21 directed the Secretary of Transportation to establish performance measures related to highway safety, asset condition, and highway system performance, among other things.[22] In addition, states and other grantees are required to establish targets related to the performance measures established by DOT and to collect data, and track progress against those targets. States and other grantees are also required to report on progress toward achieving their targets.[23] For example, beginning in 2016, states are required to report every 2 years to DOT on the progress they have made in achieving their FHWA targets.[24] Further, in 2017, 5 years after the passage of MAP-21, DOT is required to report to Congress on progress made by states and other grantees in achieving their targets. In addition to establishing a performance-based approach for existing programs under NHTSA, FHWA, and FTA, MAP-21 expanded FTA's safety oversight role and directed it to establish performance criteria for its new safety responsibilities, establish performance measures for state of good repair, develop a national transit safety plan, and develop requirements for local agency safety plans, among other things.

To implement statutory requirements, such as those contained in MAP-21, Congress has provided regulatory agencies, such as DOT, with the authority and responsibility for developing and issuing regulations. The basic process by which all federal agencies develop and issue regulations is spelled out in the Administrative Procedures Act (APA).[25] This act establishes procedures and broadly applicable federal requirements for rulemaking, including informal rulemaking, also known as notice and comment rulemaking. (See fig. 1) Among other things, the act generally requires agencies to publish a notice of proposed rulemaking in the Federal Register. After giving interested persons an opportunity to comment on the proposed rule by providing "written data, views, or arguments," the agency may then publish the final rule. In addition to the requirements under the act, proposed rules are often subject to internal and external deliberations and reviews, including official management approval within an agency, and to review and approval by the Office of Management and Budget (OMB).

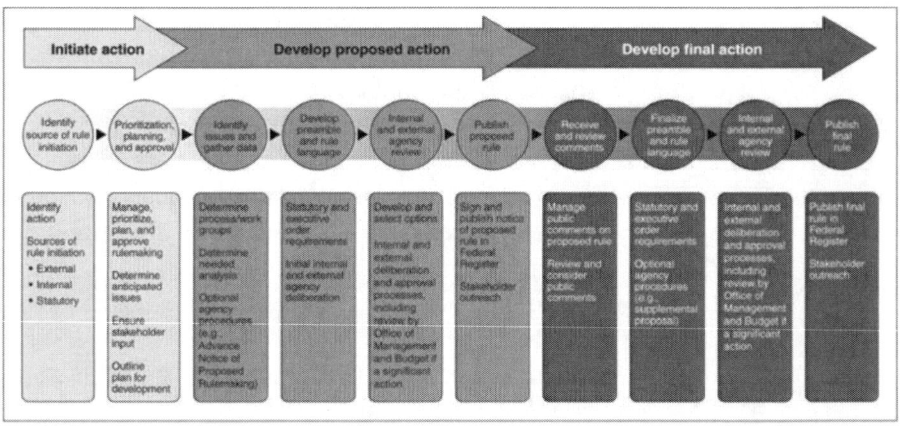

Source: GAO | GAO-15-217.

Note: The initiation of the federal rulemaking process does not always result in the publication of a final rule. For example, in some instances, agencies may develop a proposed rule, but decide to withdraw the rule later in the rulemaking process.

Figure 1. Basic Phases of the Federal Rulemaking Process.

DOT HAS MADE PROGRESS IN MOVING TOWARD A NATIONAL PERFORMANCE-BASED SYSTEM, BUT MULTIPLE FACTORS AFFECT PROGRESS

DOT Has Made Extensive Outreach Efforts to Communicate with States and Other Grantees

Since MAP-21 was enacted in July 2012, DOT has conducted an extensive outreach effort to prepare states and grantees for a national performance-based approach to surface transportation. DOT worked closely with national transportation organizations and grantees to share information and collect input about the potential performance-based requirements. DOT has:

- Established a performance working group in August 2012, comprised of FHWA, FTA, and other DOT officials as well as representatives from nine national transportation organizations. According to DOT officials, the working group, which meets on a quarterly basis, has served as a forum for DOT to coordinate outreach efforts with national organizations, and also provided national organizations with a better understanding of the potential performance-based requirements and implementation schedule.
- Conducted webinars, organized regional workshops, and facilitated peer exchanges and national organization conferences to share information with grantees.[26] For instance, FHWA and FTA sponsored a roundtable on MAP-21 during an Association of Metropolitan Planning Organizations (AMPO) conference and also participated in Transportation Research Board annual meetings.[27]
- Begun development of a technical assistance program and training curriculum on transportation performance management to assist grantees with the transition to a performance-based approach. For example, according to FHWA officials, FHWA has begun developing a technical assistance program that will include resources such as the development of guidebooks and evaluation tools, and identification of best practices. Once FHWA finalizes the rulemakings, FHWA will provide on-site assistance to its grantees through the technical assistance program. Additionally, FHWA has begun developing a training curriculum for states and MPOs that will be available once

the performance-based approach is formally established, according to FHWA officials. FHWA also conducted a national assessment of state readiness to help inform its technical assistance program and training curriculum.

- Established guidance to help communicate how certain MAP-21 performance requirements will be implemented. FHWA and FTA, for instance, jointly issued policy guidance[28] to clarify the requirement that public transportation providers must be represented on the board of MPOs that serve as transportation management areas.[29]
- Sought formal public input on potential approaches for implementing the MAP-21 requirements. For example, FTA issued an advance notice of proposed rulemaking (ANPRM), for its rules related to transit safety plans and transit asset management to solicit feedback and obtain input from grantees on the content of potential performance-based approaches to transit.

A majority of grantee officials we spoke to stated that DOT's outreach efforts have helped them understand the potential requirements and mechanics of implementing a national performance-based system. For example, officials from the New York State Association of Metropolitan Planning Organizations noted that DOT officials have provided helpful and extensive information, including responses to frequently asked questions on the FHWA website to help support the development of the performance-based approach and keep grantees informed. Similarly, officials from Washington state noted that as a result of DOT's outreach efforts, the rules that have been released for public comment have contained few unanticipated requirements.

Rules to Guide the Performance-Based Approach Are under Development

DOT is formally establishing requirements for states and other grantees to implement the performance-based approach envisioned by MAP-21 through the rulemaking process. (See table 1.) Specifically, DOT plans to establish performance measures, as well as target-setting and reporting requirements for grantees for a range of transportation activities. In some cases, MAP-21 required DOT to use the rulemaking process to implement performance-based requirements and established certain deadlines; however, in other cases, MAP-21 did not establish deadlines for implementing performance-based requirements. For example, while MAP-21 required FTA to issue a rule for target-setting and reporting requirements in transit agency safety plans, it did not establish a deadline for the issuance of a final rule. In addition, DOT officials stated that they may provide additional guidance to states and other grantees outside of the rulemaking process. For example, FTA officials stated that FTA plans to establish a National Transit Safety plan and establish minimum safety performance criteria for transit agencies as required by MAP-21, through a policy document, rather than through the formal rulemaking process.[30]

Table 1. Performance-Based Rules Planned by U.S. Department of Transportation in Response to Requirements in the Moving Ahead for Progress in the 21st Century Act (MAP-21), as of January 5, 2015

Planned rule	Agency	Description	MAP-21 rulemaking deadline, if any
Safety Performance Measure	Federal Highway Administration (FHWA)	Proposes and defines fatality and serious injury measures, along with target-setting, progress assessment, and reporting requirements.	Issue proposed rulemaking by April 1, 2014
Pavement and Bridge Performance Measure	FHWA	Proposes and defines pavement and bridge condition measures, along with target-setting, progress assessment, and reporting requirements.	Issue proposed rulemaking by April 1, 2014
Asset Management Plan	FHWA	Describes integration of pavement and bridge condition measures and other content required for asset management plans, and sets minimum standards for pavement and bridge management systems.	Issue proposed rulemaking by April 1, 2014
System Performance Measure	FHWA	Proposes and defines measures for the performance of the Interstate and non-Interstate National Highway System, traffic congestion, on-road	Issue proposed rulemaking by April 1, 2014

Table 1. (Continued)

Planned rule	Agency	Description	MAP-21 rulemaking deadline, if any
		mobile source emissions, and freight movement on the Interstate.	
Highway Safety Improvement Program	FHWA	Integrates safety performance measures into highway safety improvement program, establishes strategic highway safety plan update cycle, and updates annual reporting requirements.	Issue proposed rulemaking by October 1, 2013.
Statewide, Metropolitan and Non-Metropolitan Planning	FHWA/ Federal Transit Administration (FTA)	Establishes performance-based planning process at MPO and state level, establishes metropolitan reporting requirements, and defines coordination of target-setting.	None
Transit Asset Management	FTA	Defines state of good repair performance measures, and establishes requirements for transit asset management plan target-setting and reporting.	Issue Final Rule by October 1, 2013
Transit Agency Safety Plan	FTA	Defines transit agency safety plan content and target-setting requirements.	None
Highway Safety Program Grants	National Highway Traffic Safety Administration	Defines highway safety performance measures, target-setting, and highway safety plan content.	None[a]

Source: GAO analysis of DOT data. | GAO-15-217.

[a] To provide sufficient notice to states regarding grant application requirements for the FY 2013 and FY 2014 grant cycle, NHTSA issued an interim final rule on January 23, 2013. 78 Fed. Reg. 4986.

DOT's operating administrations have made varying degrees of progress developing their associated performance rules. (See fig. 2.) As of January 5, 2015, five out of nine rules have been available for public comment, and the remaining four rules are still under development.

- NHTSA issued an interim final rule for public comment in January 2013 but has not established a timeline for issuing a final rule. According to NHTSA officials, the agency is awaiting enactment of a new surface transportation reauthorization act before deciding on a timeframe since the timing and content of such a statute could require NHTSA to revise its interim rule.
- FHWA has released three of its five proposed rules for public comment. FHWA released two proposed rules on safety for public comment in March 2014 and is currently evaluating the comments it received.31 In addition, on January 5, 2015, FHWA released a notice of proposed rulemaking on pavement and bridge performance measures for public comment.32 FHWA plans to release its remaining two rules for public comment by April 2015.
- FTA's planned rules related to transit asset management and transit agency safety plans remain under development. FTA has not released either of its rules for public comment, although FTA did issue an ANPRM to solicit public input about the contents of its proposed rules. FTA officials said it plans to release proposed rules for transit asset management for public comment in June 2015, and a proposed rule for transit agency safety plans in August 2015.
- FTA and FHWA have jointly released for public comment a notice of proposed rulemaking related to performance-based metropolitan and statewide planning.33 The public comment period for this proposed rule closed in October 2014, and FHWA and FTA are currently evaluating the comments received on this proposed rule.

In developing these rules, DOT has missed five out of six performance-related rulemaking deadlines established in MAP-21. However, DOT officials declined to provide specific dates for when some of the rules will be finalized. FHWA plans to finalize the two safety rules and the metropolitan and statewide planning rule developed with FTA by September 2015.[34] However, FHWA has not established when its remaining rules would be finalized.

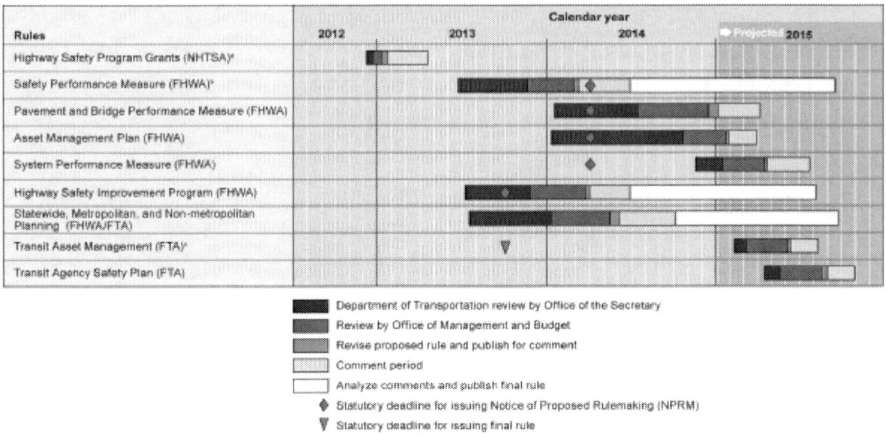

Source: GAO | GAO-15-217.

Note: DOT has not yet established a timetable for finalizing some of these rules. In these cases, this chart does not include the time estimated to finalize the rule.

[a] NHTSA = National Highway Traffic Safety Administration bFHWA = Federal Highway Administration cFTA = Federal Transit Administration.

Figure 2. Timeline for Rulemakings Implementing MAP-21 Performance-Based Approach to Surface Transportation, as of January 5, 2015.

FTA officials stated that it has not determined when its two rules would be finalized. FHWA and FTA officials we spoke with stated they could not provide a more specific date when the rulemaking process would be completed for the rules that have not yet been released for comment, noting the challenges of predicting the effect of the public comments submitted in response to its proposed rulemaking. As part of finalizing the rules, DOT plans to establish specific deadlines for grantees' implementation of the MAP-21 performance target- setting and reporting requirements. NHTSA is awaiting enactment of a new surface transportation reauthorization to see if it includes any additional requirements pertaining to its grants programs before deciding on a timeframe.

Multiple Factors Affect DOT's Progress in Developing a National Performance-Based Approach

DOT's progress in developing a national performance-based approach has been affected by the extent to which MAP-21 transformed surface transportation programs, the length and complexity of the rulemaking process, and DOT's varying levels of experience implementing a performance-based approach.

- MAP-21 began the transformation of the nature and structure of surface transportation programs by establishing a comprehensive performance-based approach for NHTSA, FHWA, and FTA, in many cases, holding states and other grantees accountable for performance for the first time. Historically, most federal surface transportation funds have been distributed through formulas that have only an indirect relationship to infrastructure needs, and many have no relationship to outcomes or grantees' performance. In general, funds have been distributed without regard to performance, and therefore, it has been difficult to determine whether federal spending has improved the performance of the nation's surface transportation infrastructure. As part of this transformational effort to shift from a process-based approach to a performance-based approach, MAP-21 required DOT to establish national performance measures that will be used by states and other grantees to set targets and report on progress in meeting those targets. However, state and grantee officials told us that in some instances, there is no broad consensus among DOT, states, MPOs, and transit grantees on how to implement a performance-based approach. While some states and grantees have been measuring performance for years, state and grantee officials we spoke with told us that their approaches have been tailored to their state and local interests and priorities, as opposed to national goals.
  In addition to moving toward a performance-based approach to surface transportation, MAP-21 created a number of new responsibilities for DOT. For example, every four years, DOT is required to review and certify the process used by each state to develop its asset management plan, which identifies strategies that help the state make progress toward its targets for asset condition, among other things. In addition, FHWA and NHTSA are responsible for evaluating and approving the process by which initial targets will be set by states in their state highway safety plans. FTA has additional responsibilities for overseeing the safety of the nation's transit system. As part of these responsibilities, FTA plans to develop an oversight approach concurrently with the development of performance measures to evaluate federal transit safety. While FTA does not have a formal role in evaluating targets related to the MAP-21 performance

measures, grantees must report to FTA on their progress meeting targets, and identify the following year's targets.

- The rulemaking process is lengthy and complex. Given the length of time a rule typically requires to be developed under the APA and extent to which MAP-21 transformed surface transportation programs, the rulemaking deadlines established by MAP-21 may have been ambitious. In our prior work, we found that rulemakings can range from 1 to nearly 14 years to complete, depending on a number of factors. More specifically, we found that a rulemaking takes an average of four years to complete, based on a sample of 16 rulemakings from four federal agencies, including DOT.[35] Within this sample, these four federal agencies took an average of about 2 1/2 years to develop and issue a proposed rule. In contrast, the timeline for MAP-21 generally gave DOT approximately 1 to 1 1/2 years to develop and issue some of the proposed rules.

  The number and extent of comments received may affect the duration and complexity of the rulemaking process. Specifically, agencies are required to respond to comments that have been received in response to a notice of proposed rulemaking.[36] We have previously found that when agencies did respond to public comments, they often made changes to the rules.[37] FHWA officials stated that they received a substantial number of comments on their safety performance measures rule, and it will take time to address these comments and revise the rule if necessary. Similarly, FTA officials stated that they received over 2500 pages of comments on FTA's ANPRM, and are reviewing and using the comments to develop FTA's transit safety and asset management plan rules. In addition, after public release of four of the five proposed rules published thus far, DOT extended the public comment period, which may delay the remaining milestones in the rulemaking process up through the publication of the final rule.

  Furthermore, DOT's rules are interrelated, so delays in establishing performance measures may cause delays in completing the process for moving to a performance-based approach. Until DOT finalizes the performance measures required by MAP-21, states and grantees will be unable to establish targets and report on progress made in relation to those performance measures. For example, three FHWA rules develop performance measures, which directly affect state target-setting and reporting requirements for grantees. (See fig. 3.) Delays in establishing performance measures may also affect information on grantee progress reported to Congress. For example, in MAP-21, Congress directed states to report biennially to DOT, beginning in October 2016, on the progress made in achieving the targets set under DOT's performance-based approach.[38] MAP-21 also directed DOT to report to Congress in October 2017 on the progress states and MPOs have made in achieving their targets. However, DOT officials acknowledged that the reports due to Congress in October 2017 may contain limited information depending on the effective dates of the MAP-21 performance requirements.

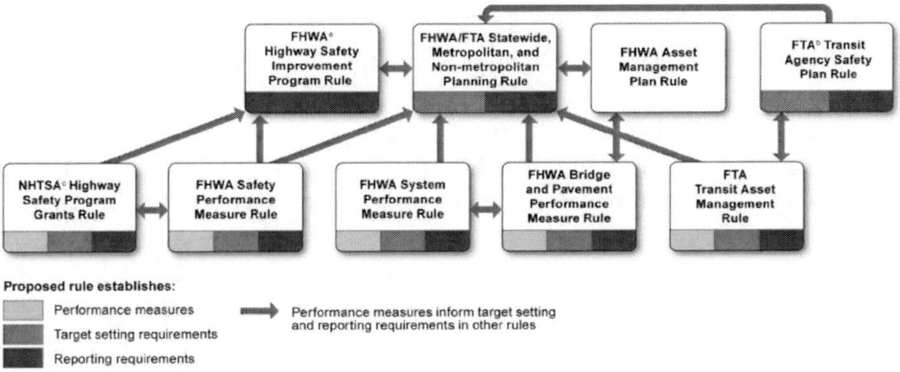

Source: GAO | GAO-15-217.

[a] FHWA = Federal Highway Administration.

[b] FTA = Federal Transit Administration.

[c] NHTSA = National Highway Traffic Safety Administration.

Figure 3. Relationships among DOT's Planned Rules Establishing a National Performance-Based Approach.

- There are varying levels of experience with performance measurement across DOT's operating administrations. For example, NHTSA has been collaborating with grantees and the Governors Highway Safety Association (GHSA) to develop performance measures in its highway safety grant programs since 2008.[39] According to NHTSA officials, in 2010, states voluntarily began reporting performance measures, targets, and progress meeting these targets in their highway safety plans. NHTSA uses these measures as a basis for reporting to Congress about highway safety. In contrast, FHWA and FTA have had more limited experience in applying a performance-based approach to its grant programs. For example, federal-aid highway program funding has historically been distributed through a complicated process based on statutory formulas. Prior to MAP-21, FTA had incorporated performance-based principles into some of its formula grant programs to allocate funding. We previously found that about 5 percent of fiscal year 2010 funding for six formula grant programs we reviewed, on average, was awarded based on transit agency performance.[40] We found that, after these grants were awarded, FTA was required to collect performance data, but FTA typically did not use the performance data to evaluate the effectiveness of its formula grant programs.[41]

Notwithstanding the factors affecting DOT's effort to implement the performance-based approach, most states and grantees we spoke with continue to take steps to implement performance-based principles into their transportation programs, though some of these grantees are awaiting further guidance from DOT. Notably, in 2014, FHWA, through its division offices, made an assessment of states' readiness to implement MAP-21 requirements and, in a draft summary report, stated that most states are actively involved and taking steps to prepare for MAP-21 implementation. State DOTs have also worked with national transportation organizations to develop criteria and broad guidelines for performance measures and to evaluate how they can be applied by members at the state or local levels. For example, officials from the American Association of State Highway and Transportation Officials (AASHTO) and state DOTs have been active in the development and deployment of transportation performance management guidelines.[42] This resulted in six overarching principles on how national-level performance measures should be developed and implemented, which guided AASHTO recommendations on these topics that were submitted to FHWA in November 2012.[43] However, a few of the grantees we spoke with stated that they are waiting for final rulemakings and rollout of national performance measures prior to implementing a performance-based approach. These officials noted that due to the uncertainty about the content of the transit-related rules, they are prioritizing local requirements over the potential MAP-21 requirements.

STATES AND OTHER GRANTEES REPORTED POTENTIAL DATA AND COST CHALLENGES TO IMPLEMENTING DOT'S PERFORMANCE-BASED APPROACH

Officials from states and other grantee agencies and representatives from national organizations we interviewed reported a variety of challenges to implementing a performance-based approach, of which data and cost challenges were most frequently cited.[44] Specifically, officials and representatives indicated data availability, collection, and analysis would be significant challenges for their agencies. Officials and representatives also frequently cited implementation costs, some associated with addressing the data challenges, although they acknowledged that they had not or could not estimate the financial impact because DOT's rulemakings have not been finalized.

States and Other Grantees Reported Potential Data Availability, Collection and Analysis Challenges

Officials and representatives we interviewed anticipated facing challenges related to the need for data, including their availability, collection and analysis. We have previously found that implementing a performance accountability framework necessitates agencies having to collect and analyze data that are useful and relevant.[45] In describing these challenges, state and other grantee officials we interviewed acknowledged that since DOT's rulemakings had not been finalized yet, it was unclear the extent to which DOT's requirements may exceed their current data and performance-based efforts.

Representatives from 5 national organizations and officials from 18 state and other grantee agencies we interviewed noted that data may not be available to measure progress, in part because there is a lack of consensus on what or how to measure certain performance areas. For example, state and grantee officials told us they were concerned that data may not be available to measure congestion, in part, because there is a lack of consensus among states and grantees regarding how to measure it. In the absence of consensus, states and other grantees have used a variety of metrics to measure congestion, which could complicate the development of national congestion measures.

Furthermore, while there has been a heightened importance placed on congestion data in rural areas due to the MAP-21 requirements and the increased freight traffic in rural areas resulting from oil and gas development, most congestion data have been historically focused on urban areas. Accordingly, a number of grantees we spoke with told us that available data sets may not reflect congestion in rural areas. In addition, some safety data may not be available. For example, while a national database for transportation fatalities exists[46], no national data source currently exists for serious injuries. Although NHTSA and GHSA developed and issued guidelines for defining serious injuries in 2012, states currently define and collect crash data differently which makes it hard to aggregate data. For example, Florida DOT officials told us their definition of a serious injury varied from other states, making their data inconsistent with other states'. In its proposed rulemaking on safety performance measures, FHWA acknowledged the need for a consistent definition of serious injuries, and proposed steps—including a system for classifying serious injuries—to address this challenge.[47]

Data collection also poses a challenge for states and grantees. Officials from 19 states and other grantees, and representatives from 6 of the national organizations we interviewed reported the following types of potential challenges associated with the data collection:

- States may have to collect additional data. For example, MAP-21 expanded the definition of the National Highway System, adding 50,000 miles including many roads owned and operated by local agencies; officials from some states noted that they have not previously collected data on these roads. In addition, FHWA has proposed that states collect data on the average annual daily traffic on all public roads. According to some state officials we spoke with, however, this would be a substantial undertaking. For example, New York DOT officials told us the state currently has adequate data for only about 37 percent of its public roads. Officials from some state DOTs also stated that they may have to collect additional data on local roads, based on their review of the requirements in FHWA's proposed rulemaking on the Highway Safety Improvement Program. For example, officials from the Montana, North Dakota, South Dakota, and Wyoming DOTs stated the requirements in FHWA's proposed rulemakings may require the collection of additional data on low-volume roads, such as all gravel and other unpaved roads in their states.

- Collecting and standardizing performance data may require additional collaboration among state and local transportation providers. For example, as part of standardizing the approach to collecting data, grantee officials from Michigan reported that it would be difficult to obtain consistent data from rural bus agencies on the condition of their assets.[48] Similarly, officials from one Florida MPO anticipated challenges in obtaining data from transit providers since the MPO has limited means for ensuring transit agencies collect and report data to them. These officials stated they are working with these transit operators to improve cooperation. Also, in order to standardize their approach to collecting data, grantees stated that they may need to revise their collection protocols. However, officials from some states suggested that this could pose a significant challenge because such protocols necessarily involve new training for agencies, such as police departments, to ensure that data is collected uniformly or could involve establishing or revising some thresholds.
- Some performance data may be proprietary and expensive to obtain from private transportation providers. We previously found that state and local officials had limited data to quantify rail-related freight impacts (such as traffic delay times or costs) on local communities.[49] State and grantee officials we interviewed suggested that they may need to obtain data from private sources, which in some cases may prove challenging. For example, according to MPO officials in Florida, freight data necessary to measure congestion (specifically on the volume of rail transport through local areas) are proprietary, and it may be difficult or expensive to access this data set from operators.[50] Similarly, officials from the New York State Association of MPOs also raised challenges about collecting performance data on freight, because of their expense and propriety nature. We have previously found that private railroads are often unwilling to provide detailed information on train counts, lengths, speed, and times to local communities to help them quantify traffic impacts at highway-grade rail crossings.[51]

Moreover, representatives from four national transportation organizations and officials from 10 states and other grantees we interviewed stated that even when data can be collected, current staffing levels, areas of expertise and data systems may not support the analyses that may be required. For example, representatives from the National Association for Regional Councils (NARC) told us that ensuring MPOs have sufficient staff capable of monitoring program performance would be a challenge. [52] We previously found that some MPOs have limited expertise or staff to analyze performance data.[53] Furthermore, during the course of our current review, officials from several MPOs told us that they rely heavily on their state DOTs to analyze data. Additionally, some state officials noted that their data systems may not be set up to report or break out analyses according to DOT's anticipated requirements. For example, South Carolina officials stated that, to conduct the analysis potentially required by DOT's rulemaking, they may need to revise their existing legacy database systems or invest in a new database system. FHWA officials have acknowledged that the data analysis capabilities of some states and grantees are limited, noting in FHWA's assessment of state readiness that 35 states may face data integration challenges and that 28 states may face data processing challenges.

While several state and other grant recipient officials we spoke with reported anticipating few or no data-related challenges, many of these officials raised concerns about how data and performance measurement would be ultimately used by DOT. Some state officials expressed concern that DOT's approach will direct states to develop targets based on outdated national data, as opposed to more current data available to the states. For example, NHTSA requires that states develop targets for highway safety based on data collected and submitted into FARS. However, the lag between when these data are collected and submitted by states and finalized by NHTSA is approximately 24 months. As a result, officials from several states, as well as AASHTO and GHSA representatives, expressed concern that states may be required to set targets based on outdated FARS data, rather than focus on setting targets based on the more current data collected by states, and that DOT would be using outdated data to determine whether states are making significant progress in meeting their targets. Officials and representatives also questioned if performance measurement should or would be tied to DOT's funding decisions, which some of them opposed, because they reported that it would be difficult to compare the transportation and transit priorities and operating environments of different states and transit agencies. Officials from several states further underscored to us that performance was a function of available funding and investments, which has not kept pace with the level of deteriorating infrastructure. Moreover, officials from some states and other grantees raised concerns that DOT's requirements might impede or hinder their approaches that have evolved over time to meet state and local needs. For example, Washington state officials anticipated that many of their existing performance management programs may be broader in scope than MAP-21 performance measures and provide more detailed information necessary to support state investment decision processes. The officials noted that the effort required to comply with the DOT national performance requirements in MAP-21 may affect the state's ability to support its own state performance measurement and investment decision process. These officials reported being concerned with how DOT will integrate legacy performance programs in states like Washington into the new framework.

DOT officials acknowledged that states and grantees will face some data challenges as part of the transition to the performance-based approach, though DOT officials noted they have taken some steps to anticipate these challenges. For example, DOT has encouraged and worked with states to share data, best practices, and templates for reporting. In addition, DOT officials stated that their overall approach has emphasized the use of existing data sets and plans to further detail its approach to ensuring data availability through its upcoming rulemakings. In addition, FHWA has used information gathered through its assessment of state readiness to help inform its technical assistance program, which DOT anticipates will address some of the above mentioned challenges.

Implementation Costs Could Vary and Be a Significant Challenge for Some States and Grantees

Representatives from 5 national organizations and officials from 22 of the 29 states and other grantees we spoke to reported potential challenges with the costs of implementing a national performance measurement system. According to FHWA officials, the total implementation costs of any one of its proposed rulemakings to states and grantees in any one year will not exceed $100 million for any one rule. For example, in March 2014, FHWA estimated the 10-year costs[54] associated with the eight new requirements proposed in its Safety Performance Measure rulemaking (see table 1) were approximately $67 million.[55] About $26 million of this is estimated to be one-time costs incurred by state DOTs and MPOs to standardize and update data collection and reporting systems, as well as the increase in level of effort from labor to establish and report targets. In calculating this cost, DOT assumed that a portion of MPOs, approximately half, would establish their own targets and that a portion would adopt state DOT targets. FHWA acknowledged that larger MPOs may have more resources available to develop performance targets and that it believed smaller MPOs (those with populations under 200,000) would have no incremental costs as they would adopt state-established targets. DOT's estimates for other rulemakings reflect the associated costs of activities (e.g., planning and data collection) beyond what is currently performed by states, MPOs, and providers of public transportation.

On a per-state or agency basis, the cost of implementation may vary depending on the characteristics of each grantee, and some states reported that these costs may exceed the average cost estimated by DOT. One MPO official reported that her organization believed DOT's estimate that the cost of administering oversight of transportation planning would increase no more than 15 percent was low. According to officials from some of the national organizations and officials from about one-third of states and grantees we interviewed, implementation costs to hire additional staff or allow for staff time and travel may be burdensome, particularly for smaller or more rural states and grantees. Officials from the New York State Association of MPOs explained that hiring and training new staff to collect and analyze performance data would require additional funding and that smaller MPOs would be more acutely affected than the larger MPOs, particularly those that do not currently conduct sophisticated analysis with the performance data. One rural transit provider we interviewed also relayed concerns about having to potentially hire an additional staff person to serve as a chief safety officer in order to meet this requirement being considered by FTA.[56] Officials from some planning organizations we interviewed underscored their lack of planning professionals and how the few individuals employed by their agencies were already responsible for fulfilling multiple roles.

Implementation costs may also vary by grantees' experience in different surface transportation areas. In summer 2014, FHWA queried its division offices about the readiness of states to implement performance-based approaches to transportation projects in their states. According to the division offices, in the areas of congestion, air quality and freight, only 20 to 40 percent of states had adopted performance management practices, and only about 10 to 20 percent of states are very highly prepared to carry out performance-based programs in these areas. For example, in Nevada, FHWA officials reported that state officials may need some additional assistance to integrate data and develop metrics for congestion, freight, and air quality. On the other hand, state DOTs and other grantees may be better positioned to meet DOT's performance measurement requirements in other areas, such as safety, pavement, and bridge condition. According to FHWA's assessment, about 40 to 50 percent of the states are ready to carry out a performance-based program in some areas, such as safety, pavement, and bridge condition, where, historically, measures and targets have been used by states to evaluate program performance. According to the division offices, in these areas about 60 to 70 percent of the states integrate performance into their long-range plans, develop quantifiable targets to guide investment decision making, and develop plans that document their strategies to achieve targets.

According to AASHTO, some of its members have concerns that collecting data to support these rules may reduce the portion of their federal highway grants available to fund transportation projects over the long term. While these costs are eligible for federal planning funds, officials from several grantee agencies said they do not expect additional federal funding for implementation. Representatives from several national organizations and officials from some states and other grantees we interviewed emphasized that DOT should, whenever possible, leverage existing resources or data or procure data sources itself. Representatives from the American Public Transportation Association suggested that DOT consider the data that it will be asking transit agencies to collect, pointing to recent FTA-sponsored asset management pilot projects that demonstrated the data collection process can be burdensome and should be based on the types of information that states and local transit agencies currently collect.[57] Similarly, representatives from the National Association of Development Organizations also underscored the cost of acquiring and analyzing data and the need to structure data collection around existing sources. DOT officials agreed that data availability, collection, analysis and associated costs present potential challenges, and stated that in order to address this situation, DOT has emphasized the use of existing data sets and intends to further detail its approach to ensuring data availability through its upcoming rulemakings.

CONCLUDING OBSERVATIONS

DOT's effort to develop a performance-based approach for its various surface transportation grant recipients represents a significant shift for the Department, transforming the federal involvement in surface transportation to a more outcome-oriented approach, as we have recommended since 2008. In many cases, the shift to a performance-based approach will hold states and other grantees accountable for performance for the first time. Such an approach could provide a strong foundation for holding grant recipients responsible for achieving federal objectives and measuring overall program performance. However, the development and implementation of a performance-based approach is not without challenges. Notably, as NHTSA's implementation of a performance-based approach has demonstrated, this broader effort of incorporating performance-based principles into the overall surface transportation program may take longer than Congress originally anticipated. In addition, while many grantees have been evaluating the performance of transportation projects for many years, experiences with performance measurement varies and even the most experienced grantees may face challenges aligning their individual approaches with DOT's national approach. Nevertheless, given the billions of dollars provided annually in federal funding to improve the nation's highway and transit infrastructure and safety—and competing demands for that funding—the ability to assess the outcomes of federal surface transportation programs and hold grant recipients accountable for results could help all parties more efficiently allocate federal funds to address specific challenges and areas of concern.

Agency Comments

We provided a draft of this report to DOT for review and comment. DOT provided technical comments, which we incorporated as appropriate. We are sending copies of this report to interested congressional committees and the Secretary of Transportation.

Susan Fleming
Director, Physical Infrastructure

Appendix I: Objectives, Scope, and Methodology

The objectives of our review were to determine: (1) the progress that DOT has made in developing a national performance-based approach to surface transportation and (2) the challenges states and other grantees report facing in implementing this approach.

To address these objectives, we reviewed scholarly/peer-reviewed, government, trade, and non-profit literature from 2011 through 2014, the time period just before and since MAP-21 was enacted. The reviewed literature included those published by the National Cooperative Highway Research

Program, which is sponsored by FHWA and American Association of State Highway and Transportation Officials (AASHTO) and presented at the Transportation Research Board annual conference. The literature examined local and national transportation performance based approaches. We also reviewed DOT-conducted performance management case studies and workshop summaries and reports that were publicly available, as well as, our body of work on performance management in the federal government and transportation programs.

To examine the progress that DOT has made in developing a national performance-based approach for surface transportation programs, we reviewed related requirements and timetables in MAP-21 for FHWA, FTA, and NHTSA as well as interim and proposed rulemakings developed by these operating administrations in response to these requirements.[1] We did not evaluate the potential effectiveness of the proposed rules because the content may change before rules are finalized in response to comments submitted by grantees and other parties. We also analyzed DOT documents, information obtained through interviews with DOT officials, guidance issued through the rulemaking process, and information from grantee interviews. We also analyzed information from the Report on DOT Significant Rulemakings, issued monthly, which provides the original, actual, and projected dates for the major milestones in the rulemaking process to understand the progress FHWA, FTA, and NHTSA have made developing the performance-based approach. In the event that actual dates were unavailable, projected dates, obtained directly from the Report on DOT Significant Rulemakings were used to calculate the length of milestones. We interviewed FHWA, FTA, and NHTSA officials to understand the factors affecting DOT's progress in developing the performance-based approach.

To understand the challenges states and other grantees face in implementing a performance-based approach to surface transportation, we analyzed comments submitted to DOT by and interviewed representatives from seven national transportation organizations (such as AASHTO, Association of Metropolitan Planning Organizations, and American Public Transportation Association), which broadly represent state and local transportation, transit, and planning interests and perspectives, both in urban and rural communities.

We also reviewed the comments submitted to DOT and conducted semi-structured interviews with state and local officials from 29 grantee agencies in 13 states—Florida, Maryland, Michigan, Montana, New York, North Dakota, Oregon, South Carolina, South Dakota, Virginia, Washington, Wyoming, and Utah. We developed criteria—population growth trends, population size, geographic location, transit infrastructure age, and experiences managing and measuring transportation project performance—which we used to select a cross-section of grantee agencies (i.e., state transportation agencies, state highway safety offices, metropolitan and rural planning organizations, and transit agencies). We also relied on suggestions from trade organizations and DOT to identify agencies that would meet our criteria and to identify specific state and local officials. Based on these criteria, in four states, we interviewed officials from the state department of transportation, one or more metropolitan planning organizations, local transit providers, and DOT regional oversight offices;[2] in the remaining nine states, we interviewed officials from at least one state transportation agency, planning organization or transit agency in that state. In addition to discussing anticipated challenges, state and grantee officials also provided information about state and local transportation planning processes, the experience and extent of available performance management data, and DOT's progress to date with its outreach and rulemaking. The results of interviews with state and local officials from these 29 grantee agencies cannot be generalized to all federal transportation grantees; however, they provided insight into the types of challenges that some grantees anticipate in implementing DOT's future rulemaking and overall performance based approach, as well as, perspectives on DOT's outreach and rulemaking progress.

To further understand the challenges that states and other grantees may face, we also reviewed the draft results of a questionnaire DOT administered to its 52 FHWA Division Offices assessing states' readiness to implement a performance-based approach. This questionnaire was administered from July through August 2014, and its purpose was to assist FHWA in how to best design program support for states in meeting requirements under DOT's future performance-based approach.

We conducted this performance audit from May 2014 to January 2015 in accordance with generally accepted government auditing standards. Those standards require that we plan and perform the audit to obtain sufficient, appropriate evidence to provide a reasonable basis for our findings and conclusions based on our audit objectives. We believe that the evidence obtained provides a reasonable basis for our findings and conclusions based on our audit objectives.

APPENDIX II: DEPARTMENT OF TRANSPORTATION RULEMAKINGS FOR SELECTED MAP-21 PERFORMANCE REQUIREMENTS

Table 2. Federal Highway Administration's (FHWA) Proposed Rulemakings Incorporating Selected MAP-21 Performance Requirements

Proposed rulemakings	Requirement	Source of requirement
Safety Performance Measure (comment period for rule closed)	Department of Transportation (DOT) to establish measures for states to assess serious injuries and fatalities per vehicle mile traveled and the number of serious injuries and fatalities.	23 U.S.C. § 150(c)(4)
	States and metropolitan planning organizations (MPOs) to establish targets for DOT-defined performance measures on serious injuries and fatalities per vehicle mile traveled and the number of serious injuries and fatalities.	23 U.S.C. § 150(d), 134(h)(2), 135(d)(2)
	States to report biennially to DOT on National Highway System condition and performance, the progress made toward the achievement of targets, and the effectiveness of the investment strategy document in the state asset management plan.	23 U.S.C. § 150(e)
	States to achieve or make significant progress toward the achievement of targets to carry out the Highway Safety Improvement Program.	23 U.S.C. § 148(i)
Pavement and Bridge Performance Measure Rule (open for public comment)	DOT to establish measures to assess the condition of pavements on the Interstate and National Highway System and the condition of bridges on the National Highway System.	23 U.S.C. § 150(c)(3)
	States and MPOs to establish targets for the condition of pavements on the Interstate and National Highway System and the condition of bridges on the National Highway System.	23 U.S.C. §§ 150(d), 134(h)(2),135(d)(2)
	States to report biennially to FHWA on National Highway System condition and performance, the progress made toward the achievement of targets, and the effectiveness	23 U.S.C. § 150(e)

Table 2. (Continued)

Proposed rulemakings	Requirement	Source of requirement
	of the investment strategy document in the state asset management plan.	
	States to achieve or make significant progress toward the achievement of targets to carry out the National Highway Performance Program.	23 U.S.C. § 119 (e)(7)
	Penalty is imposed on states that do not maintain a minimum condition on roads on the Interstate System.	23 U.S.C. § 119 (f)(1)(A)
	Penalty is imposed on states that do not maintain a minimum condition for bridges on the National Highway System.	23 U.S.C. § 119 (f)(2)(A)
Asset Management Plan Rule (rule under development)	DOT shall establish minimum standards for States to use in developing and operating bridge and pavement management systems.	23 U.S.C. § 150(c)(3)(A)(i)
	DOT to establish requirements for state asset management plans.	23 U.S.C. § 119(e)(8)
	States to develop an asset management plan for National Highway System pavement and bridges.	23 U.S.C. § 119(e)
System Performance Measure Rule (rule under development)	DOT to establish measures for states to assess the performance of the Interstate and non-Interstate National Highway System, traffic congestion, on-road mobile source emissions, and freight movement on the interstate.	23 U.S.C. § 150(c)(5), (6)
	States and MPOs to establish targets for DOT-defined measures for the performance of the Interstate and non-Interstate National Highway System, traffic congestion, on-road mobile source emissions, and freight movement on the interstate.	23 U.S.C. §§ 150(d), 134(h)(2), 135(d)(2)
	Metropolitan planning organizations serving a transportation management area over 1 million in population representing a nonattainment or maintenance area to develop a new Congestion Mitigation and Air Quality Improvement Program (CMAQ) performance plan.	23 U.S.C. § 149(l)
	States to report biennially to FHWA on highway condition and performance, the progress made toward the achievement of	23 U.S.C. § 150(e)

Proposed rulemakings	Requirement	Source of requirement
	targets, the effectiveness of the investment strategy document in the state asset management plan, and addressing congestion at freight bottlenecks.	
	States to achieve or make significant progress toward the achievement of targets set under the National Highway Performance Program.	23 U.S.C. § 119 (e)(7)
Highway Safety Improvement Program Rule (comment period for rule closed)	DOT to establish requirements for state updates of strategic highway safety plan and states will update their respective plans.	23 U.S.C. § 148(d)
	States to report to FHWA on the results of highway safety improvement projects and the progress towards achieving targets.	23 U.S.C. § 148(h)
Statewide Metropolitan Planning Rule (comment period for rule closed)[a]	Metropolitan planning organizations (MPOs) and states coordinate to integrate the goals, objectives, performance measures, and targets into the planning process.	23 U.S.C. §§ 135(d)(2), 134(h)(2); 49 U.S.C. §§ 5303(h)(2), 5304(d)(2);
	Metropolitan and statewide improvement program, to the maximum extent practicable, to include information on how the planned programs will achieve targets set by the state and MPOs.	23 U.S.C. §§ 134(j)(2)(D),135(g)(4); 49 U.S.C. §§ 5303(j)(2)(D), 5304(g)(4)
	MPOs to provide a system performance report to document progress.	23 U.S.C. § 134(i)(2)(C); 49 U.S.C. § 5303(i)(2)(C)
	DOT to establish criteria to evaluate the effectiveness of the performance-based planning process of states, considering the extent to which States are making progress toward achieving their targets developing appropriate targets.	23 U.S.C. § 135(h)(1); 49 U.S.C. § 5304(h)(1);

Source: GAO analysis of DOT information. | GAO-15-217

[a] The Statewide, Metropolitan, and Non-Metropolitan Planning rulemaking has been developed jointly with the Federal Transit Administration.

Table 3. Federal Transit Administration's Proposed and Planned Rules Incorporating Selected MAP-21 Performance Requirements

Proposed rulemakings	Requirement	Source of requirement
Transit Asset Management Rule (rule under development)	DOT to establish performance measures for transit agencies based on transit state of good repair standards.	49 U.S.C. § 5326(c)(1)
	Public transportation federal fund recipients to develop transit asset management plans.	49 U.S.C. § 5326(b)(2)
	Public transportation federal fund recipients to establish targets for measures established by DOT based on the state of good repair standards.	49 U.S.C. § 5326(c)(2)
	Direct recipients of public transportation federal funding assistance to report to FTA on progress in achieving transit targets.	49 U.S.C. § 5326(c)(3)
Transit Agency Safety Plan Rule (rule under development)	Public transportation federal fund recipients (or states) to include targets based on the safety performance criteria and state of good repair standards established by DOT.	49 U.S.C. § 5329(d)(1)(E)
	Public transportation federal fund recipients (or states) to develop a transit safety plan.	49 U.S.C. § 5329(d)(1)

Source: GAO analysis of DOT information. | GAO-15-217.

Table 4. National Highway Traffic Safety Administration's Proposed and Planned Rules Incorporating Selected MAP-21 Performance Requirements

Interim rulemaking	Requirement	Source of requirement
Highway Safety Program Grants Rule (interim rule issued)	States to include highway safety measures in state Highway Safety Plans	23 U.S.C. § 402(k)(3)(A),(4)
	States to establish targets for the performance measures required to be included in the state's Highway Safety Plan.	23 U.S.C. § 402(k)(3)(A)(ii)
	States to submit an annual Highway Safety Plan.	23 U.S.C. § 402(k)
	States to annually report to DOT on progress in meeting safety performance targets in the Highway Safety Plan.	23 U.S.C. § 402(k)(3)(E)
	DOT to submit biennial reports to Congress	23 U.S.C. §

Interim rulemaking	Requirement	Source of requirement
	evaluating each state's performance with respect to the Highway Safety Plan and performance targets, and any recommendations for improvements.	402(n)

Source: GAO analysis of DOT information. | GAO-15-217.

End Notes

[1] Metropolitan planning organizations are defined in federal legislation as the designated local decision-making body that is responsible for carrying out the transportation planning process in metropolitan areas. A metropolitan planning organization must be designated for each urbanized area with a population of 50,000 or more.

[2] GAO, Surface Transportation: Restructured Federal Approach Needed for More Focused, Performance-Based, and Sustainable Programs, GAO-08-400 (Washington, D.C.: Mar. 6, 2008).

[3] GAO, High-Risk Series: An Update, GAO-13-283 (Washington, D.C.: Feb. 2013).

[4] Pub. L. No. 112-141, §§ 1106, 1203, 20019,20021, 126 Stat. 405, 432-437, 524-527, 708 (2012), adding 23 U.S.C. § 150 (national goals and performance management measures for highway systems, including bridges and tunnels) and 49 U.S.C. § 5326 (transit asset management, including goals and performance measures), and amending 23 U.S.C. §§ 119 (national highway performance program), 134 (metropolitan transportation planning), 135 (statewide and nonmetropolitan transportation planning), 148 (highway safety improvement), 149 (congestion mitigation and air quality improvement), 402 (state highway safety programs), and 49 U.S.C. §§ 5303 (metropolitan transportation planning) 5304 (statewide and nonmetropolitan transportation planning), 5310(h) (enhanced mobility of seniors and individuals with disabilities), among others.

[5] The National Highway System (NHS) consists of approximately 220,000 miles of the nearly 1-million miles of roadways eligible for federal-aid. It includes the 47,000-mile Interstate Highway System as well as other roadways, arterials, and connectors important to U.S. strategic defense policy, and connects to major intermodal facilities, such as airports or transit hubs.

[6] 23 U.S.C. § 119(e)(7), (f). See also 23 U.S.C. § 148(i).

[7] Highway and Transportation Funding Act of 2014, Pub. L. No. 113-159, 128 Stat. 1839 (2014).

[8] In this review, we analyzed the MAP-21 performance provisions that applied to FHWA, FTA, and NHTSA. We did not review the performance provisions associated with the Federal Motor Carrier Safety Administration (FMCSA) because there were no requirements in MAP-21 for DOT to develop formal rules related to FMCSA's grantees' performance. In addition, we did not review the MAP-21 requirement that directed FTA to submit a report to Congress regarding performance measures pertinent to grants for the enhanced mobility of seniors and individuals with disabilities. 49 U.S.C. § 5310(h).

[9] These states were Florida, Michigan, New York, and South Carolina. We did not interview a transit provider in South Carolina.

[10] The remaining 7 percent of FHWA's budget includes approximately $2.5 billion (6 percent) for other highway programs—including the Transportation Infrastructure Finance and Innovation program, the Federal Lands Highway program, and highway funding to U.S. territories, among other things—and $400 million (1 percent) for administrative expenses.

[11] According to FHWA, about 2,300 of its 2,900 staff work on the federal-aid highway program. The remaining 600 staff are associated with other FHWA programs, including the Federal Lands Highway Program.

[12] For federally required state and metropolitan planning processes, see 23 U.S.C. §§ 134- 135 and 49 U.S.C. §§ 5303-5305.

[13] 23 U.S.C. § 135(g)(7) and 23 C.F.R. § 450.218 (a).

[14] GAO, Statewide Transportation Planning: Opportunities Exist to Transition to Performance-Based Planning and Oversight, GAO-11-77 (Washington, D.C.: Dec. 15, 2010).

[15] Historically, grant funds distributed through FHWA's federal-aid highway program have been distributed using a series of complex formulas that take into account a number of factors, including the estimated share of taxes highway users in each state contributed to the fund, among other things. See GAO, Highway Trust Fund: All States Received More Funding Than They Contributed in Highway Taxes from 2005 to 2009, GAO-11-918 (Washington, D.C.: Sept. 8, 2011).

[16] GAO, Federal Transit Programs: Federal Transit Administration Has Opportunities to Improve Performance Accountability, GAO-11-54 (Washington, D.C.: Nov. 17, 2010).

[17] GAO-11-77.

[18] GAO-11-77.

[19] GAO-08-400.

[20] GAO-08-400.

[21] GAO, Managing for Results: Executive Branch Should More Fully Implement the GPRA Modernization Act to Address Pressing Governance Challenges, GAO-13-518 (Washington, D.C.: June 26, 2013).

[22] Additional information on selected performance requirements contained in MAP-21 for FHWA, FTA, NHTSA and their applicable grantees is provided in appendix II.

[23] 23 U.S.C. § 150(e) and 49 U.S.C. § 5326(c)(3).

[24] Specifically, beginning in 2016 and biennially thereafter, MAP-21 directed states to report to DOT on the progress they have made in achieving targets established in relation to the following performance measures: the condition of pavements on the Interstate System and National Highway Systems; the condition of bridges on the National Highway System, the performance of the Interstate System and National Highway System; the number of serious injuries and fatalities, in total and per vehicle mile traveled; serious injuries and fatalities per vehicle mile traveled and in total; traffic congestion; on-road mobile source emissions; and freight movement on the Interstate system. 23 U.S.C. § 150(e).

[25] Pub. L. No. 404, 60 Stat. 237 (1946), codified at 5 U.S.C. ch. 5.

[26] According to DOT officials, a peer exchange is an opportunity for transportation planning staff to interact, share information, accomplishments, and lessons learned from the field and develop approaches to overcome shared transportation planning challenges. The peer exchanges look to advance the state of practice in multimodal transportation planning nationwide by organizing, facilitating, and documenting peer events to share noteworthy practices among state DOTs, MPOs, transit agencies, and local and tribal transportation planning agencies.

[27] AMPO is a national member-based organization that provides MPOs with technical assistance and training, conferences and workshops, and research among other services. The

Transportation Research Board (TRB), one of six major divisions of the National Research Council, is a private, nonprofit institution. The TRB provides services to government agencies and the public as well as to the scientific and engineering communities.

[28] See 79 Fed. Reg. 31214 (June 2, 2014).

[29] A transportation management area is an urbanized area with a population greater than 200,000, based on the 2010 census. If requested by the Governor and the MPO in the area, an area with a population less than 200,000 can also be designated as a transportation management area. 23 U.S.C. § 134(k).

[30] FTA officials stated that while the National Transit Safety plan will be established outside of the rulemaking process, the plan will still be subject to public notice and comment.

[31] 79 Fed. Reg. 17464 (Mar. 28, 2014); 79 Fed. Reg. 13846 (Mar. 11, 2014).

[32] 80 Fed. Reg. 326 (Jan. 5, 2015).

[33] 79 Fed. Reg. 31784 (Jun. 2, 2014).

[34] Specifically, as discussed in DOT's December 2014 Report on DOT Significant Rulemakings, FHWA planned to finalize the Highway Safety Improvement Program rule in August 2015, and the Safety Performance Measure and Statewide, Metropolitan, and Non-metropolitan rules in September 2015.

[35] GAO, Federal Rulemaking: Improvements Needed to Monitoring and Evaluation of Rules Development as Well as to the Transparency of OMB Regulatory Reviews, GAO-09-205 (Washington, D.C.: Apr. 20, 2009).

[36] GAO, Federal Rulemaking: Agencies Could Take Additional Steps to Respond to Public Comments, GAO-13-21, (Washington, D.C.: December 2012).

[37] GAO-13-21.

[38] 23 U.S.C. §150.

[39] GHSA, a national transportation organization, represents the state and territorial highway safety offices that are responsible for implementing programs to address behavioral highway safety issues.

[40] GAO, Federal Transit Programs: Federal Transit Administration Has Opportunities to Improve Performance Accountability, GAO-11-54 (Washington, D.C.: Nov. 17, 2010).

[41] GAO-11-54. We recommended, among other things, that FTA study and report to Congress on options for adding performance accountability mechanisms to transit grant programs. DOT agreed to consider our recommendation.

[42] AASHTO is a nonprofit, nonpartisan association. AASHTO represents highway and transportation departments in the 50 states, the District of Columbia, and Puerto Rico. AASHTO also represents all five transportation modes: air, highways, public transportation, rail, and water. AASHTO's stated primary goal is to foster the development, operation, and maintenance of an integrated national transportation system.

[43] These principles include, among other things, that initial national-level performance measures should build on existing performance measures, management practices, data sets, and reporting processes. Another principle is that national-level performance measures should focus on areas and assets over which state DOTs have control.

[44] Officials and representatives also reported other challenges to a lesser extent including coordination or planning between local stakeholders and target setting.

[45] GAO-11-54.

[46] The Fatality Analysis Reporting System (FARS) is a data collection system that provides a census of all fatal traffic crashes in the United States. FARS data provides support for most of the traffic and highway safety programs aimed at reducing the number of fatalities on the Nation's highways. These data are collected on a purely voluntary basis through

cooperative agreements between NHTSA and each of the 50 States, the District of Columbia, and Puerto Rico.

[47] 79 Fed. Reg. 13846 (Mar. 11, 2014).

[48] According to a Michigan DOT official, the agency currently collects service miles, service hours, and age of vehicle on rural transit vehicles, and it would be difficult to collect consistent condition data, such as a condition rating or performance rating for each vehicle or the fleet as a whole.

[49] GAO. Freight Transportation: Developing National Strategy Would Benefit from Added Focus on Community Congestion Impacts, GAO-14-740 (Washington, D.C.: Sept. 19, 2014).

[50] MAP-21 includes a goal to reduce congestion—which could incorporate local traffic congestion caused by freight flows—and a goal to reduce the environmental impacts of freight movement on the national freight network. For more information, see GAO-14-740.

[51] GAO-14-740.

[52] NARC is a national member-based organization that provides information and research on key national policy issues and federal policy developments. The association conducts training sessions, conferences, workshops and webinars for its members which include regional councils, metropolitan planning organizations, and other entities.

[53] GAO, Metropolitan Planning Organizations: Options Exist to Enhance Transportation Planning Capacity and Federal Oversight, GAO-09-868, (Washington, D.C.: Sept. 9, 2009).

[54] This figure represents undiscounted incremental costs.

[55] According to FHWA, it could not directly quantify the expected benefits due to data limitations and the nature of the benefits from the proposed rule. Therefore, in order to evaluate benefits, FHWA used a break-even analysis as the primary approach to quantify benefits. Following this approach, FHWA used the break-even analysis to assess the level of reduction in fatalities or incapacitating injuries needed for the benefits to justify the costs of the proposed rule. The results of the break-even analysis showed that the proposed rule would need to prevent approximately 7 fatalities or an equivalent 153 incapacitating injuries nationwide over 10 years to generate enough benefits to outweigh the cost of the proposed rule.

[56] FTA's ANPRM for its planned transit performance rules sought input on the need for public transportation providers to identify a chief safety officer who reports to a general manager or equivalent.

[57] FTA conducted these pilot projects in California, Idaho, Illinois, Massachusetts, and Utah.

End Notes for Appendix I

[1] In this review, we analyzed the MAP-21 performance provisions that applied to FHWA, FTA and NHTSA. We did not review the performance provisions associated with the Federal Motor Carrier Safety Administration (FMCSA) because there were no requirements in MAP-21 for DOT to develop formal rules related to FMCSA's grantees' performance. In addition, we did not review the MAP-21 requirement that directed FTA to submit a report to Congress regarding performance measures pertinent to grants for the enhanced mobility of seniors and individuals with disabilities. (49 U.S.C. § 5310(h)).

[2] These four states were Florida, Michigan, New York, and South Carolina. We did not interview a transit provider in South Carolina.

In: Performance-Based Transportation Programs ISBN: 978-1-63482-722-5
Editor: Travis Schmidt

Chapter 2

FEDERAL TRANSIT PROGRAMS: FEDERAL TRANSIT ADMINISTRATION HAS OPPORTUNITIES TO IMPROVE PERFORMANCE ACCOUNTABILITY*

United States Government Accountability Office

WHY GAO DID THIS STUDY

Public demand and federal funding for transit have grown in recent years, yet most of this funding is not tied to performance. As Congress prepares for reauthorization of the federal surface transportation programs, GAO was asked to report on (1) the extent to which federal transit programs use performance information in making decisions about funding distribution and in evaluating the programs' effectiveness; (2) mechanisms for making these programs more performance based, and strategies for supporting their successful implementation; and (3) how selected U.S. and foreign transit agencies have used performance measurement in their planning and decisions, and their views on the federal role in transit. To do so, GAO analyzed legislation, federal documents, and literature; interviewed federal officials and transit experts; and conducted semistructured interviews with selected transit

* This is an edited, reformatted and augmented version of a United States Government Accountability Office publication, No. November 2010., dated GAO-11-54.

agencies using criteria that, for U.S. agencies, covered a variety of regions and population sizes and, for foreign agencies, multiple transit modes and English language capability.

What GAO Recommends

The Federal Transit Administration (FTA) should (1) report to Congress on options for adding performance accountability mechanisms to transit programs to ensure efficient and effective federal transit programs and (2) further analyze and use transit agency data, when applicable, for evaluating federal transit program performance. DOT reviewed a draft of this report, provided technical clarifications, and said it would consider our recommendations.

What GAO Found

Some federal transit programs distribute funds based partly on performance, but opportunities to improve grant recipients' performance accountability remain. Of the eight transit programs GAO reviewed—which represent 97 percent of total federal transit grants in fiscal year 2010 (excluding funds provided under the American Recovery and Reinvestment Act)—two are generally funded by congressional direction, while the remaining six are funded through legislatively defined grant formulas. Federal funding for the two nonformula programs GAO reviewed—the New Starts Program and the Bus and Bus Related Equipment and Facilities Program—is awarded in part according to performance. A small percentage of federal transit funding for the six formula programs is apportioned based on performance—according to GAO's analysis, about 5 percent, on average, of fiscal year 2010 funding. FTA does not, in general, analyze fully or use the performance data it collects from transit agencies to evaluate the effectiveness of its transit grant programs; thus, FTA is missing a valuable opportunity to evaluate the end results of its program activities and programs' funding formulas.

GAO identified three performance accountability mechanisms for making federal transit programs more performance based, including providing financial rewards or penalties/sanctions, increasing or decreasing program flexibility as a performance incentive, and recognizing entities that achieve certain performance goals. These mechanisms have both potential advantages—most notably, they can encourage improved performance and help agencies make sound decisions when allocating limited funds—and potential disadvantages that can produce inequitable results or burden transit agencies with requirements to gather, maintain, and analyze data. GAO also identified several key strategies that can support the use of these mechanisms and mitigate their disadvantages, such as ensuring that mechanisms are of sufficient value and that appropriate measures are selected, among others. However, without FTA analysis of the appropriateness, feasibility, and potential impact of using various transit performance mechanisms, Congress may lack information to determine whether and how these mechanisms could be used to make transit funding more performance based as it prepares for the upcoming surface transportation reauthorization.

Transit agencies that GAO interviewed use performance measurement to varying degrees, but they face challenges in linking performance with planning and decision making. All of these agencies measure performance in certain categories, such as ridership and on-time performance, but the extent to which they measure it in others—such as environmental impact, energy usage, and economic development—varies widely. Transit agency officials reported that measuring performance presents challenges, in part because it can be difficult to obtain relevant data and develop a sound methodology. They also said that linking performance to planning and decision making is challenging because of either limited funding or political priorities. These transit agencies and other experts suggested a variety of changes to the federal role in transit, including increasing investment in existing transit infrastructure; developing federal transit program goals that generally address broader issues, such as encouraging a shift from automobiles to public transit; and promoting livable communities around transit systems.

ABBREVIATIONS

APTA	American Public Transportation Association
FTA	Federal Transit Administration
DOT	Department of Transportation
GPRA	Government Performance and Results Act of 1993
HSIP	Highway Safety Improvement Plan
JARC	Job Access and Reverse Commute

MPO	metropolitan planning organization
NHTSA	National Highway Traffic Safety Administration
NTD	National Transit Database
OVAE	Office of Vocational and Adult Education
POP	Program of Projects
SAFETEA-LU	Safe, Accountable, Flexible, Efficient Transportation Equity Act: A Legacy for Users
STIC	Small Transit Intensive Cities
TRB	Transportation Review Board

* * *

November 17, 2010

The Honorable Christopher J. Dodd
Chairman

The Honorable Richard C. Shelby
Ranking Member
Committee on Banking, Housing, and Urban Affairs
United States Senate

Public transit systems provide an important source of mobility for many Americans while also helping to alleviate traffic congestion and provide environmental benefits. From 1999 to 2009, ridership on transit systems in the United States grew nearly 16 percent to reach about 10.25 billion, and despite the recent economic recession, demand for public transit has remained near record levels, reaching a peak of 10.4 billion passenger trips in 2008. Recent economic pressures have, however, contributed to flat or reduced funding for many transit agencies, as well as service cuts and higher fares.[1] With demand for transit service near record levels, the federal investment in transit needs to be accompanied by strong performance accountability to ensure that funds are being used efficiently and effectively. We have previously raised concerns about the lack of performance accountability in federal transportation programs, including transit, and have called for steps to enhance the accountability of federal investments in transportation infrastructure.[2]

The Safe, Accountable, Flexible, Efficient Transportation Equity Act: A Legacy for Users (SAFETEA-LU), enacted in August 2005, authorized over $286 billion for federal surface transportation programs from fiscal years 2005 through 2009, including more than $52 billion for federal transit programs, a 46 percent increase over the previous funding authorization for transit programs.[3] The Surface Transportation Extension Act of 2010 extended the funding authorization for SAFETEA-LU programs through December 31, 2010.[4] Congress and the administration are currently debating reauthorization of the entire surface transportation program, including transit programs. In preparation for this reauthorization, the Department of Transportation (DOT) recently conducted a series of "listening sessions" with key stakeholders and interested citizens to obtain their views. DOT plans to issue a detailed proposal for a surface transportation reauthorization bill in February 2011.

While federal funding for transit has increased significantly in recent years, most of this spending is not explicitly linked to performance. In light of this, you asked us to examine ways to make federal transit programs more performance based. Accordingly, this report addresses the following questions: (1) To what extent do federal transit programs use performance information in making decisions about distributing funds and in evaluating the effectiveness of transit programs? (2) What mechanisms exist for making federal transit programs more performance based, including their potential advantages and disadvantages, and what strategies exist for supporting their successful implementation? (3) How have selected U.S. and foreign transit agencies incorporated performance measurement into their planning and decision making, and what are these agencies' views on the federal role in transit?

To address the first objective, we reviewed 8 of the 18 federal transit programs. These 8 programs account for nearly 97 percent of all Federal Transit Administration (FTA) grant funds, excluding funds provided under the American Recovery and Reinvestment Act.[5] We analyzed pertinent federal legislation and reports, including SAFETEA-LU, the Government Performance and Results Act of 1993 (GPRA),[6] and FTA documents on grants programs that distribute transit funds. We interviewed FTA officials to determine the extent to which performance measurement/outcomes are factors in funding formulas and decisions. We also compared FTA's practices with performance system criteria found in GPRA, Transportation Research Board (TRB) reports, and other sources. To simulate incentive tier apportionments for formula programs, we analyzed FTA apportionment documents and National Transit Database (NTD) data. To address the second objective, we reviewed and synthesized literature— including GAO, FTA, TRB, and other transportation reports—and interviewed transit agency officials and industry experts to describe what mechanisms exist for making federal transit programs more performance based, the advantages and disadvantages of those mechanisms, and the strategies that exist for overcoming disadvantages. Finally, to describe how selected U.S. and foreign transit agencies incorporate performance measurement into their planning and decision making and their views on the federal role in transit, we conducted semistructured interviews with 10 U.S. transit agencies, selected to ensure geographic distribution and variation in the size of the population served, as well as 2 foreign transit agencies, selected, in part, based on the number of transportation modes offered by their system. The information we gathered from these agencies, however, cannot be generalized across all U.S. or foreign transit agencies. We also conducted interviews with industry experts to obtain their views on how transit agencies incorporate performance measurement into funding and strategic decisions.

We conducted this performance audit from November 2009 through November 2010 in accordance with generally accepted government auditing standards. Those standards require that we plan and perform the audit to obtain sufficient, appropriate evidence to provide a reasonable basis for our findings and conclusions based on our audit objectives. We believe that the evidence obtained provides a reasonable basis for our findings and conclusions based on our audit objectives. See appendix I for more information about our scope and methodology.

BACKGROUND

Federal Transit Programs

Federal transit funds are distributed to recipients by formula, through specific designations within the legislation, or on a discretionary basis through individual grant programs. FTA administers its programs according to the programmatic framework for the nation's transportation infrastructure specified in SAFETEA-LU. FTA works in partnership with the states and other grant recipients to administer federal transit programs, providing financial assistance, policy direction, technical expertise, and some oversight. State and local governments are ultimately responsible for executing most federal transit programs by matching and distributing federal funds and by planning, selecting, and supervising infrastructure projects and safety programs—all in accordance with federal requirements. The eight federal transit programs we reviewed, which represent 97 percent of FTA's total fiscal year 2010 grant funds (excluding funds provided under the American Recovery and Reinvestment Act) and their respective goals are as follows:

- **The Urbanized Area Formula Grant Program** makes funding available to urbanized areas and to states for public transportation capital projects and operating assistance for equipment and facilities in urbanized areas and for transportation-related planning.[7] Funds are allocated based on a multitiered formula, which separates urban areas with populations under 200,000 from those with populations of 200,000 or more. Funds are first apportioned based on a formula provided in law to designated recipients (typically metropolitan planning organizations [MPO] or a state or regional authority that is responsible for capital projects and for financing and directly providing public transportation).[8] Designated recipients allocate the apportionment among eligible transit service providers in the urbanized area, and then transit providers may submit grant applications to FTA.[9]
- **The Nonurbanized Area Formula Grant Program** provides funding to states and Indian tribes for the purpose of supporting public transportation capital projects and operating costs for equipment and facilities in rural areas with populations of less than 50,000. Funds are first apportioned to states and Indian tribes based on a formula provided in law, then states and Indian tribes may submit applications to FTA.[10] Grant recipients may allocate funds to state or local governmental authorities, or an operator of public transportation or intercity bus service.
- **The Fixed-Guideway Modernization Program** makes federal resources available for the purposes of modernizing or improving existing fixed-guideway systems.[11] Funds are first apportioned to urbanized areas according to a seven-tier formula. Public transit entities (transit authorities and other state and local governmental authorities) in those urbanized areas to which the funds are apportioned may submit applications to FTA.[12]
- **The Bus and Bus Related Equipment and Facilities Program** provides capital assistance for new and replacement buses, related equipment, and facilities for expansion and maintenance purposes. The projects funded by this program are generally determined by Congress. Funds may be provided only to state and local governmental authorities. The Bus Testing Facility Program—which

has a single facility for testing new bus models for maintainability, reliability, safety, performance, and other factors—is also administered under this program.[13]

- **The New Starts Program** provides funds for construction of new fixed-guideway systems or extensions to existing fixed-guideway systems. These grants are awarded for specific projects by congressional directive based on FTA recommendations. Funds may be provided only to state and local governmental authorities.[14]
- **The New Freedom Program** provides funding for capital and operating expenses for new public transportation services and alternatives beyond those required by the Americans with Disabilities Act of 1990 that are designed to assist individuals with disabilities.[15] Funds are first apportioned to designated recipients and states based on a formula provided in law. Designated recipients and states to which funds have been apportioned may submit grant applications to FTA.[16] The recipients of these grants, in cooperation with the MPO, are responsible for conducting an areawide competitive solicitation for grant applications from subrecipients (i.e.: state and local governmental authorities, private nonprofit organizations, or transit service operators).[17]
- **The Job Access and Reverse Commute (JARC) Program** provides funding for capital, planning, and operating expenses for projects that transport low-income individuals to and from jobs and activities related to employment and for reverse commute projects. Funds are first apportioned to designated recipients and states based on a formula provided in law. Designated recipients and states to which the funds have been apportioned may submit grant applications to FTA.[18] The recipients of these grants, in cooperation with the MPO, are responsible for conducting an areawide competitive solicitation for grant applications from subrecipients (i.e.: state and local governmental authorities, private nonprofit organizations, or transit service operators).[19]
- **The Special Needs of Elderly Individuals and Individuals with Disabilities Program** provides funding to states for the purpose of assisting private nonprofit groups in meeting the transportation needs of elderly individuals and individuals with disabilities when current transportation services are unavailable, insufficient, or inappropriate for meeting these needs. Funds are first apportioned to states based on a formula administered by the Secretary of Transportation that

> considers the number of elderly individuals and individuals with disabilities in each state. States forward an annual Program of Projects (POP) and grant applications to FTA.[20] States may allocate apportioned funds to a private nonprofit organization[21] or a governmental authority.[22]

While most people in the United States travel by motor vehicle, demand for public transit continues to grow. According to the U.S. Census Bureau, the number of people who commute to work using public transit grew by about 1 million from 2005 to 2008 to reach approximately 7.21 million persons. Annual federal, state, and local investment in transit grew nearly 77 percent between 1997 and 2006 to total almost $31 billion. During the recent economic recession, however, investment in transit did not keep pace with demand, according to the American Public Transportation Association (APTA), a leading industry organization. Moreover, according to a March 2010 survey conducted by APTA, because of the economic downturn, more than half of the country's largest transit agencies have recently cut service and/or raised fares and many are also facing budget shortfalls in 2011.[23]

Transit organizations vary widely in size from large systems with multiple modes of transportation, such as the New York City Metropolitan Transit Authority, to smaller organizations, including single-vehicle paratransit services.[24]

The governance structure for these organizations varies and includes, among others, entities that are units or departments of (1) city, county, or local governments; (2) state governments; (3) private for-profit corporations; and (4) university or college systems.

PERFORMANCE ACCOUNTABILITY

Accountability for performance varies from grant program to grant program. For the purposes of this report, performance accountability is defined as the mechanisms by which individuals or organizations are held accountable for meeting specified performance-related expectations, such as goals. Performance measurement is the ongoing monitoring and reporting of program accomplishments, particularly progress toward established goals. In this report, we have focused on specific mechanisms that are meant to encourage performance—such as rewards given or penalties imposed.

GPRA requires agencies governmentwide to establish agency and program goals and performance measures, and to report on their results in achieving those goals for all their program activities, including grant programs. Performance measures may address the type or level of program activities conducted (process-oriented measures), the direct products and services delivered by a program (output-oriented measures), and/or the results of those products and services (outcome-oriented measures). Performance information, for the purposes of this report, refers to data on performance resulting from performance measurement.

To improve both grant performance and grantee performance accountability, Congress, granting agencies, and grantees can use performance accountability mechanisms, which are provisions or specific actions that can be taken at different points in the grant life cycle.[25]

SOME FEDERAL TRANSIT PROGRAMS DISTRIBUTE FUNDS BASED PARTLY ON PERFORMANCE, BUT OPPORTUNITIES TO IMPROVE GRANT RECIPIENTS' PERFORMANCE ACCOUNTABILITY REMAIN

Of the eight SAFETEA-LU transit programs we reviewed, two are generally funded by congressional direction, while the remaining six are funded through legislatively defined grant formulas.

Funding for Nonformula Programs under SAFETEA-LU, Including New Starts, Is Based Partly on Performance

Funding for the New Starts Program and the Bus and Bus Related Equipment and Facilities Program—the two non-formula-based SAFETEALU programs we reviewed—is based partly on performance.

- New Starts is often cited as a model for other federal transportation programs because its grant evaluation process is used to distinguish among proposed investments, though GAO and others have also identified challenges related to the complexity and cost of this process.[26] New Starts funding is allocated by Congress to specific projects according to FTA's recommendations to Congress. FTA's recommendations are based on statutorily identified criteria such as projected performance on land use, cost effectiveness, and other criteria. By necessity, the New Starts proposed projects are evaluated based on *projected* performance on the selected criteria, rather than actual performance, because the projects have not yet started.

- For the Bus and Bus Related Equipment and Facilities Program, funding is generally directed by Congress, except most recently in fiscal year 2007, when, according to agency officials, FTA allocated funding in part based on transit agency performance on ridership and bus load (i.e., actual ridership as compared with total capacity).

Only a Small Percentage of Federal Transit Funding for Formula Programs under SAFETEA-LU Is Awarded Based on Performance Considerations

According to our analysis, the SAFETEA-LU formulas require that about 5 percent, on average, of fiscal year 2010 funding be awarded based on transit agency performance for the six formula programs we reviewed (see table 1). The remaining grant funding distribution is based on infrastructure-related factors, such as total route miles and revenue vehicle miles, or demographic factors, as shown in table 1.

Performance measures include measures of costs per passenger mile or vehicle revenue miles per capita because they measure agencies' activities against capacity, demand, or costs. To illustrate this, using the example of costs per passenger mile, an agency with low costs that is also providing a low level of service (i.e., a low number of passenger miles) is not performing as well as an agency with comparable population and population density that is able to provide a high number of passenger miles while keeping costs per passenger mile low.

One of the six formula grant programs we reviewed—the Urbanized Area Formula Grant—bases funding, in part, on performance, per statutory requirements,[27] while the other five formula programs we reviewed are funded entirely based on demographic and infrastructure-related factors as shown in table 1.

Table 1. Fiscal Year 2010 Apportionment Factors and Average Percentage of Funding Based on Performance for FTA Formula Transit Programs

Program		**Apportionment factors**	**Averagepercentage offunding based onperformancea**
Urbanized Area Formula	Performance-related factors	**Areas under 200,000 in population** •Passenger miles traveled per vehicle revenue mile •Passenger miles traveled per vehicle revenue hour •Vehicle revenue miles per capita •Vehicle revenue hours per capita •Passenger miles traveled per capita •Passenger trips per capita **Areas with population of 200,000 or greater** •Fixed-guideway passenger miles times fixed-guideway passenger miles/operating cost •Bus passenger miles times bus passenger miles/operating cost	7.82
	Non-performance-related factors	**Areas under 200,000 in population** •Population •Actual population multiplied by population density (measure of actual population and population per mile)	

Program		Apportionment factors	Averagepercentage offunding based onperformancea
		Areas with population of 200,000 or greater •Population •Actual population multiplied by population density (measure of actual population and population per mile) •Revenue vehicle miles •Route miles	
Fixed-Guideway Modernization		•Route miles •Revenue vehicle miles	0
New Freedom		•Ratio of population of individuals with disabilities in each eligible area to the populations of individuals with disabilities in all eligible areas	0
Job Access and Reverse Commute		•Ratio of low-income individuals and welfare recipients in each eligible area to number of low-income individuals and welfare recipients in all eligible areas	0
Nonurbanized Area Formula		•Ratio of nonurbanized population in each state to the nonurbanized population of all of the states •Ratio of nonurbanized land area in each state to the nonurbanized land area of all of the states	0

Table 1. (Continued)

Program		Apportionment factors	Averagepercentage offunding based onperformancea
Special Needs of Elderly Individuals and Individuals with Disabilities		•Population of elderly individuals and individuals with disabilities	0
Total formula funding based on performance			4.87

Source: GAO analysis of fiscal year 2010 FTA appropriations and FTA grant formula documents.

Note: Because the New Starts and Bus and Bus Related Equipment and Facilities program grants are either awarded on a discretionary basis or directed by Congress, they have been excluded from this analysis. While these grant programs are based in part on performance, we were not able to quantify the extent to which performance was considered for these grant programs.

[a]Percentages are the average for all agencies. The actual percentage of funding based on performance will vary by agency depending on individual data.

Under the Urbanized Area Formula Grant Program, approximately 8 percent of the funding, on average, is apportioned based on transit agency performance, although the actual percentage of an individual transit agency's funding based on performance varies. This program apportions funds to two groups of agencies, as follows:

- For transit agencies in urbanized areas with populations under 200,000, (small cities), funding is apportioned based mostly on demographic data. However, urbanized areas may be eligible for additional incentive funding, which is apportioned in the following way: For each of six performance measures for which the urbanized area performs above the average performance of larger urbanized areas, small city urbanized areas may receive additional funding in the apportionment.[28] In the end, only 1 percent of total funding for this grant program is apportioned in this way.
- For urbanized areas with populations of 200,000 or greater, funding is apportioned in part based on infrastructure-related measures and in part through an incentive tier measuring passenger miles per dollar of operating costs.[29] The remaining 7 percent of performance-based funding for this program is apportioned in this way. However, the incentive for an agency to change its behavior to increase its grant apportionment is small compared with its operating costs. GAO's simulations of the incentive tier apportionment show that a 10 percent increase in an urbanized area's passenger miles (while holding the area's operating costs and data for all other urbanized areas constant) typically results in additional funding of less than 0.5 percent of operating costs for the area. Several aspects of the design of the transit formula incentive tier contribute to the relatively small size of the incentive available to a transit agency. First, the overall level of funding apportioned under the incentive tier is relatively small, both as a fraction of total federal aid for the Urbanized Area Formula Grant Program and also as a fraction of current operating expenses. Second, because all the transit agencies within an urbanized area are included in the passenger miles and operating costs of the urbanized area, the incentive apportionment to a single transit agency may be affected by changes in the behavior of other agencies within the urbanized area. Additionally, even if a transit agency's increased performance results in an increased apportionment amount for the urbanized area, there is no guarantee that that transit agency will benefit from the increased

apportionment, as the designated recipient is responsible for allocating the apportioned funds among area agencies.[30] As we discuss later in this report, when an incentive is not of sufficient value, the expected return does not outweigh the expected risk or costs, and recipients are not motivated to pursue the performance improvement.

Once Grants Are Awarded, FTA Collects Performance Information on the Programs as Required, but Generally Does Not Use Performance Data to Evaluate the Effectiveness of FTA's Grant Programs

FTA has developed some performance measures and targets related to DOT's strategic goals. Some of these strategic goals and performance measures are related to internal DOT and FTA performance (e.g., organizational excellence); others relate to how well DOT and FTA programs are performing. FTA tracks performance against a set target. For example, in DOT's *Performance and Accountability Report* and FTA's budget documents, FTA provides information on the following goals and measures:[31]

- Related to DOT's safety goal, FTA measures transit fatalities and injuries per 100 million passenger-miles traveled.
- Related to DOT's reduced congestion goal, FTA measures the average percentage change in ridership for the 150 largest transit agencies, as well as the percentage of bus fleets and rail stations compliant with the Americans with Disability Act of 1990.[32]
- Also related to DOT's reduced congestion goal, FTA measures the number of jobs made accessible by the JARC program.

In addition to measuring and reporting performance in these areas, FTA has implemented several initiatives aimed at improving grantee performance. For instance, FTA's Transit State of Good Repair program, which focuses on ensuring that local transit systems are maintained in a state of good repair, initiated a national discussion about the condition of the nation's infrastructure as an issue posing pressing challenges for most of the nation's transit systems. The goals of this initiative are to raise awareness of state of good repair issues throughout the industry, bring stakeholders together to assess and measure the scope of maintenance problems, and explore creative approaches to financing necessary repairs and upgrades for aging transportation assets. Additionally,

FTA recognizes high-performing transit agencies with nonfinancial awards through various programs. For example, through 2008, FTA recognized transit agencies that experienced significant increases in public transportation ridership. The program was suspended in 2009 in response to the overall trend of decreasing ridership.

FTA also collects performance data from about 2,000 transit agencies through the National Transit Database (NTD)[33] and other reporting requirements.[34] The reporting requirements vary somewhat by program, as follows:

- Recipients of Urbanized Area Formula Grants and Nonurbanized Area Formula Grants are required to submit information on performance and other information to the National Transit Database. This includes information on ridership, vehicle revenue miles, vehicle information (such as the age and type of the vehicle), and financial information, among other categories.
- Recipients of several other transit grants are required to report performance information specific to the goals of the program to help FTA fulfill its obligations under GPRA.[35] For example, recipients of the Special Needs of Elderly Individuals and Individuals with Disabilities grants are required to report data on gaps in service filled and rides provided for elderly individuals or individuals with disabilities as a result of the grant.[36] JARC recipients are required to report information on the number of jobs made accessible and the number of rides provided as a result of JARC funding.[37] Recipients of the New Freedom grant program are required to report on services and rides provided to individuals with disabilities and changes made to infrastructure, technology, or vehicles that affect the availability of transportation services as a result of the New Freedom projects implemented in the current reporting year.[38]

FTA has set targets for some broad goals and has some initiatives aimed at increasing grantee performance, but does not, in general, use the performance data it collects to evaluate the effectiveness of its grant programs. FTA officials stated that FTA's strategic goals and objectives are generally determined based on their relationship to DOT's strategic goals as well as the priorities of senior FTA officials. We have previously reported that agencies can use performance information to, among other things, identify problems or weaknesses in programs, to try to identify factors causing the problems, and to modify a service or process to try to address problems.[39] FTA officials use collected performance data to track overall program trends and performance on a national level, but not to determine the link between specific FTA program activities and changes in performance. For example, FTA reports performance statistics to Congress through its biennial report, *Status of the Nation's Highways, Bridges, and Transit: Conditions and Performance*.[40] This report includes the change over time for statistics such as average operating speed, vehicle use statistics, frequency and reliability of services, condition of transit assets and infrastructure, and safety, among others. However, FTA does not explore the potential reasons for a change in performance over time. Similarly, FTA officials stated that FTA does not conduct analysis of changes in transit agency performance or set targets for the measures that are incentivized in grant formulas to determine what effect incentives have on transit agency performance (i.e., the extent to which the incentive funding is having the desired outcome). As a result, FTA is missing a valuable opportunity to evaluate the end results of its program activities and SAFETEA-LU funding formulas. Information on the effectiveness of formula incentive programs, in particular, is necessary for determining how and when to make changes to funding mechanisms in the future.

PERFORMANCE ACCOUNTABILITY MECHANISMS CAN IMPROVE PERFORMANCE OF TRANSIT AGENCIES, AND ALTHOUGH THEY POTENTIALLY PRESENT DISADVANTAGES, MOST OF THESE CAN BE MITIGATED BY FOLLOWING KEY STRATEGIES

Potential Advantages of Using Performance Accountability Mechanisms Are Encouraging Good Performance, Deterring Poor Performance, and Helping Agencies Allocate Limited Funds

Through our literature review, we identified major financial and nonfinancial mechanisms for making federal transit programs more performance based. Tables 2 and 3 describe the three types of mechanisms we found and their potential advantages and provide examples of how various federal and state agencies or programs use them.

Table 2. Types and Descriptions of Financial Mechanisms, Their Potential Advantages, and Examples of Use

Type and description of financial mechanisms	Potential advantages	Examples
Financial rewards or penalties/sanctions These types of mechanisms involve an increase or decrease in funding. •Entire amount can be tied to performance, or a portion of funding above an established baseline (i.e., an incentive portion). •A onetime cash bonus payment or a onetime reduction in payment penalty. •Longer-term increases or decreases in the funding term, per unit reimbursement rate, or overall funding levels. •Financial sanctions may also be imposed in one area to influence actions in another area (crossover sanctions). Ideally, under these financial mechanisms, program funds are allocated based on the achievement of performance goals by •establishing a performance-based formula, •providing bonus funding including the use of performance incentives, or •imposing additional eligibility requirements for funding (e.g., requiring grant recipients to develop performance plans).	Provides positive financial motivation for organizations to change their behavior and encourages them to accomplish goals to obtain additional funding. Creates clear links between performance and funding and helps hold grant recipients accountable for achieving desired results and outcomes. Financial penalties or sanctions penalize organizations financially for not meeting requirements and are intended to help agencies make sound decisions when allocating limited funds.	Department of Education's grants for vocational education[a] These grants provide financial rewards and impose financial penalties based on performance.[b] States are eligible to receive incentive funds if they exceed performance goals for these grants. States not meeting their performance levels for 2 years are subject to financial sanctions, although no state has failed to meet its overall goals for 2 consecutive years. Highway Safety Improvement Program (HSIP) In implementing HSIP, SAFETEA-LU required state transportation departments to prepare strategic highway safety plans.[c] The plans were to address several key elements, including evaluating and measuring states' performance toward the overall goal of reducing traffic fatalities.[d] The states were required to submit their plans to avoid incurring a financial penalty totheir HSIP funds.[e] State Safety Oversight Program[f]

Table 2. (Continued)

Type and description of financial mechanisms	Potential advantages	Examples
		Under this program, FTA requires states to designate an agency to oversee the safety and security of rail transit systems that receive federalfunding. State oversight agencies are responsiblefor developing program standards that transit agencies must meet and reviewing the performance of the transit agencies against thosestandards. For example, the state oversight agency must establish a safety program plan that outlines oversight and transit agency responsibilities, review transit agencies' safety and security plans, conduct safety and security audits, and investigate accidents. If a state has not met the requirements of the State Safety Oversight Program, FTA may withhold up to 5 percent of the state's appropriated funds for the Urbanized Area Formula Grant Program.[g]

Type and description of financial mechanisms	Potential advantages	Examples
		Virginia Department of Transportation Highway Maintenance[h] Budgets are tied to performance targets established for maintaining each of the assets. Performance targets are expressed as a percentage of assets meeting or exceeding the desired condition level. Funding is allocated based on the desired system (asset) condition.

Source: GAO.

[a]The Office of Vocational and Adult Education (OVAE) administers the federal vocational education grants that are authorized by the Carl D. Perkins Vocational and Technical Education Act of 1998 (Perkins III). Perkins III defines major roles for OVAE and states in establishing performance accountability systems for vocational and technical education.

[b]States are responsible for developing performance goals and measures and data collection systems related to four required core performance indicators: academic and technical skill attainment, course completion, job placement and retention, and nontraditional participation and completion.

[c]23 U.S.C. § 148.

[d]The plans were to address four key elements: (1) eight types of stakeholders must participate in preparing the plan, (2) the plan must define areas of safety emphasis through an analysis of state fatality and serious injury data, (3) the plan must identify strategies and projects that cover all aspects of highway safety (infrastructure, behavioral, and emergency medical services), and (4) the plan must provide for evaluating and measuring states' performance toward the overall goal of reducing traffic fatalities.

[e]SAFETEA-LU added a requirement that states without a strategic plan in place by October 2007 would still receive funds for highway safety improvement, but the amount would be capped at the fiscal year 2007 level.

[f]49 U.S.C. § 5330: 49 C.F.R. Part 659.

[g]FTA may agree to restore withheld formula funds if compliance is achieved within two years. See, 49 C.F.R. § 659.7.

[h]Virginia's transportation system, the third largest in the nation, is composed of 124,000 lane miles, over 12,000 bridges, four underwater crossings, two mountain tunnels, four ferries, and a portfolio of parking lots and rest areas. Responding to increasing pressures to understand the condition, remaining useful life, funding needed for replacement/repair, and performance targets for its assets, the department developed an asset management system that it uses to track and measure maintenance performance.

Table 3. Type and Description of Nonfinancial Mechanisms, Their Potential Advantages, and Examples of Use

Type and description of nonfinancial mechanisms	Potential advantages	Examples
Increase or decrease program flexibility as a performance incentive Increase or decrease in grantee's flexibility by issuing administrative, programmatic, or financial waivers from requirements and restrictions or by adding award conditions	Encourages good performance and may enhance grantee's ability to use innovation in directing resources where needed to solve problems	National Highway Traffic Safety Administration (NHTSA) SAFETEA-LU established penalties for states that fail to enact federally required laws to reduce the number of alcohol-related fatalities associated with (1) repeat drunk driving offendersaand (2) open alcoholic beverage containers in motor vehicles.bStates that failed to adopt these required laws were penalized byhaving a portion of their federal highway construction funds transferred to highway safety programs. The Environmental Protection Agencyaffords states with high environmental performance levels greater flexibility in spending their grant funds, as part of the National Environmental Performance Partnership System.
Recognize those entities that achieve certain performance goals Public recognition of good performance, for example, through the press, Web sites, intranets, newsletters, hearings, testimony, and award ceremonies	Encourages and rewards good performance through public recognition	Federal Interagency Coordinating Council on Access and Mobility's United We Ride Initiativeimplemented national community leadership awards for transportation coordination. These are nonmonetary awards that recognize states, localities, communities, or organizations that have provided leadership and action toward developing and/or implementing exemplary high-quality coordinated human service transportation programs or systems.

Source: GAO.

[a] 23 U.S.C. § 164.

[b] 23 U.S.C. § 154.

In short, these mechanisms create a link between performance and benefits by either rewarding good performance or penalizing poor performance. However, the extent to which a reward or penalty motivates performance depends on its importance to the agency—if a financial reward or penalty is too small, for example, it may not affect behavior. At the same time, a reward that is too small to influence a large agency may be significant to a smaller agency.

Potential Disadvantages to Using Performance Mechanisms Are That They Can Burden Transit Agencies, Produce Inequitable Results, and Raise Other Concerns

Our literature review found not only advantages associated with performance accountability mechanisms but some potential downsides and concerns as well.

- Most notably, to demonstrate that an incentive has been achieved or that a penalty is not warranted, **agencies have to gather, maintain, and analyze data, and these tasks require resources**. Therefore, to the extent possible, the measure on which an incentive or penalty is awarded or assessed should be based on readily available information, or information that could be readily obtained. If not, it could place a burden on the agency's resources.
- Additionally, when penalizing organizations for not meeting requirements, there are concerns that **(1) an organization may be penalized before it has a chance to address its performance problems, and (2) a punitive approach to performance accountability may be taken rather than a constructive approach.** For example, even if penalties are employed to promote performance accountability, there should be a constructive, collaborative approach to performance improvement that both precedes and follows the penalty.

  Our literature review also identified other disadvantages that relate specifically to implementing financial performance accountability mechanisms. These include the following:
- **The zero-sum nature of performance-based allocations, particularly under constrained resources, can cause inequity, as programs can improve and still receive nothing.** For example, all

recipients might improve their performance, so that those improving the least might not be rewarded. Also, under resource constraints, performance-based allocations are not likely to provide a meaningful incentive to improve performance or may not be possible. For instance, a basic reason behind tying the allocation of funding to performance is that this will provide an incentive for funding recipients to perform better (to either generate additional funds or avoid financial penalties). However, according to a 2004 study on the use of performance standards and measures for public transportation systems, there is not much evidence that the various formulas used to fund transit agencies actually produce this result.[41] One reason is that even if a single transit system were to make significant performance improvements, the current apportionment formulas do not result in much of a funding change from year to year (in part because of the fact that the change in one system is but a small fraction of the statewide or nationwide numbers that feed into the formulas).

- **Well-funded grant recipients, with the staff and resources to implement more sweeping changes, may be rewarded at the expense of poorly funded ones that may have more pressing operational concerns.** Moreover, for poorly funded recipients, the amount of improvements required may not be realistically attainable through changes within the recipients' control. For example, according to the previously mentioned study done in 2004, some transit agencies would like to see an increase in the funding provided from local, as opposed to state and federal, sources.[42] However, a funding stream that includes a requirement for contribution of local dollars could be particularly difficult to accomplish for rural systems with limited revenue or for systems where local leaders do not support a contribution of local dollars.[43] This could result in a transit system being penalized financially for a decision made outside its control, with an ensuing decline in service quality. To be fair, factors well beyond the control of the transit agency are often drivers of performance (e.g., local economic problems leading to a drop in employment that in turn leads to a drop in ridership).
- **Grant recipients may be charged with meeting conflicting goals.** For example, if an important local goal for a transit agency is to increase geographic service coverage, the achievement of this goal might have negative impacts on performance as commonly defined—efficiency and/or effectiveness. For a transit system that wants to

develop new evening or weekend service, generally such service will be less productive than weekday service. Performance-based funding is likely to provide a disincentive for providing such service.[44]

- If not designed correctly, **performance mechanisms can introduce perverse incentives**. For example, regarding a federal employment program that has used incentive awards—the Workforce Investment Act's Title I-B Program for Dislocated Workers—we reported in 2009 that local agency officials receiving grants under the program may be reluctant to provide services to job seekers that are less likely to find and maintain a job, because the incentive award is tied to achieving performance levels in placement and retention.[45] This is contrary to the program's objective, which is to assist all job seekers in obtaining employment.

Finally, when considering the use of performance accountability mechanisms for transit agencies, DOT officials noted that transit grant recipients operate within the context of their local, state, and regional government structures and funding sources. Therefore, some changes may need to be enacted by other organizations to improve transit service, and it may be appropriate to provide incentives to these other government structures as well.

Key Strategies Can Help Overcome Some Disadvantages of Performance Accountability Mechanisms and Help Ensure Successful Implementation of Those Mechanisms

Our earlier work discusses how five key strategies collectively facilitate the effective selection, design, and implementation of performance accountability mechanisms.[46] They are as follows:

1) Ensure mechanisms are of sufficient value. The value of the rewards and penalties—whether financial or nonfinancial—and the cost of improved performance are adequate to motivate desired behaviors and provide a meaningful return to both the grantor and the grantee.
2) Periodically renegotiate and revise mechanisms and measures. Provide for and use the flexibility to reevaluate performance accountability mechanisms and associated performance measures at regular, scheduled intervals and allow time to learn from each cycle to improve performance.

3) Ensure appropriate measures are selected. Measures should represent performance that is within the grantee's sphere of influence, and can reasonably be achieved and evaluated within the specified time frame, and should be tested over time to minimize the potential for unintended consequences and perverse incentives. Additionally, performance data should be tested and validated to make sure they are credible, reliable, and valid. Absent these attributes, organizations lack the basis for sound decisions about rewards and penalties.
4) Ensure grantor and grantee technical capacity. Grantors and grantees should have the necessary knowledge about performance accountability mechanisms and the ability to effectively implement them.
5) Ensure phased implementation. Allow time to design, test, and revise measurement systems before linking them to accountability mechanisms.

These five key strategies can help mitigate the disadvantages we have previously discussed related to using performance accountability mechanisms, as shown in table 4.

Table 4. Disadvantages of Performance Accountability Mechanisms and How Key Strategies Can Help Overcome Them

Disadvantages of mechanism	Strategies for overcoming disadvantages
• Agencies have to gather, maintain, and analyze data, and these tasks require resources.	• Ensure appropriate measures are selected. The performance measure on which the incentive is awarded should be based on readily available information, or information that could be readily obtained. • Ensure phased implementation. The use of performance factors in allocating funds could be phased in over several years to make sure the data collection methods and application of the measures are accurate and well understood by all parties.

Table 4. (Continued)

Disadvantages of mechanism	Strategies for overcoming disadvantages
• An organization may be penalized before it has a chance to address its performance problems, and a punitive approach to performance accountability may be taken rather than a constructive approach.	• Ensure grantor and grantee technical capacity. Grantors should help recipients solve their performance problems before being financially penalized. • Ensure phased implementation. The introduction of performance factors could be phased in over several years to make sure the data collection methods and application of the measures are accurate and well understood by all parties. Additionally, phased implementation would allow for agencies to measure performance and correct any performance issues before being financially penalized.
• The zero-sum nature of performance-based allocations can cause inequity, as programs can improve and still receive nothing.	• Ensure mechanisms are of sufficient value. To the extent that a goal of performance-based funding is to motivate better performance, if the performance component of funding is to be effective, it must be large enough to motivate behavior.
• Well-funded grant recipients may be rewarded at the expense of poorly funded ones.	• Ensure appropriate measures are selected. Choose measures thatare within the program recipients' sphere of influence and test the performance targets to ensure they are attainable.
• Grant recipients may be charged with meeting conflicting goals.	• Ensure appropriate measures are selected. Choose measures thatare within the program recipients' sphere of influence and test the performance targets to ensure they are attainable.
• Performance mechanisms can introduce perverse incentives.	• Ensuring appropriate measures are selected could mitigate the risk of creating perverse incentives. Measures should be carefully linked to program goals.

Source: GAO analysis.

Some of these strategies address multiple disadvantages. For example, table 4 shows that ensuring appropriate measures are selected could mitigate four of the six disadvantages. In addition, we found in our literature review that to ensure financial stability, many sources advocated for providing transit agencies with a baseline funding amount that would enable grantees to know the minimum (or a baseline amount) that they would receive each year, and then providing additional funds that would be based on performance. Although not a key strategy, this more specific option would help address the following three disadvantages: the zero-sum nature of performance-based allocations, well-funded grant recipients being rewarded at the expense of poorly funded ones, and grant recipients being charged with meeting conflicting goals.

Appropriateness of and Success in Using Performance Accountability Mechanisms Depend on Program Goals, but Little Is Known about Using These Mechanisms in Transit Programs

Although performance mechanisms can provide advantages, and the disadvantages can be mitigated, they are still not suitable for all programs. As previously discussed, the eight federal transit programs that we reviewed are designed to accomplish different goals, and the use of performance accountability mechanisms is better suited to some than to others. For example, discretionary grant programs such as New Starts, which are designed to award funds to the best potential performers, may be better suited to the use of performance accountability mechanisms, while formula programs, such as the Urbanized Area Formula Grant Program and Fixed-Guideway Modernization Program, which are intended to support the financial stability of transit agencies or distributional equity, may be less well suited. We have found that performance accountability mechanisms need to be tailored to specific situations, since not all mechanisms are appropriate to all situations, and there is no "one-size-fitsall" solution to performance accountability.[47] Furthermore, according to FTA, transit systems vary in size, resources, and community needs, making it less productive to judge all systems on a common set of performance measures or performance accountability mechanisms.

Even though mechanisms are not all appropriate for all situations, performance accountability mechanisms still hold promise. As we have described in the previous section of this report, DOT is requiring some transportation grants to be based on performance, with good results in some departments. For example, NHTSA used performance information on alcohol-related injuries and fatalities to target grant funding and specific program strategies to states with the highest impaired driver rates. However, DOT has only required transit grants to be minimally based on performance. Expanding the use of performance accountability mechanisms in the area of transit could help make transit grants more performance based. The performance accountability mechanisms described in this report suggest opportunities for

FTA to study their impact and potentially use them to make transit grants more performance based—i.e., to identify grantee performance problems, look for solutions, and make other important management decisions, per leading practices.[48] Congress also has a role to play in increasing the use of performance mechanisms in transit, as part of its process of setting national priorities and allocating the resources to achieve them. Congress has a number of opportunities to initiate the use of performance mechanisms, such as when it establishes or reauthorizes a program, during the annual appropriations process, and during hearings focused on program and agency operations. Moreover, our 2006 report on performance accountability mechanisms recommended that the federal Office of Management and Budget encourage and assist federal agencies in working with Congress to expand the effective use of performance accountability mechanisms when federal grant programs are being created or reauthorized. As noted earlier in this report, Congress and the administration are currently debating reauthorization of the entire surface transportation program, including transit programs. However, without FTA analysis of the appropriateness, feasibility, and potential impact of using various transit performance mechanisms, Congress may lack the information needed to identify and implement the most effective mechanisms and better help transit agencies maximize their potential. Furthermore, because each mechanism may not be suited to every program, such analysis may require careful study to ensure the best link between mechanisms and transit programs.

Selected Transit Agencies Use Performance Measurement to Varying Degrees and See a Role for the Federal Government in Transit but Cited Challenges in Linking Performance with Planning and Decision Making

All Transit Agencies We Interviewed Measure Performance in Some Categories, but the Extent to Which They Measure It in Others Varies Widely

While officials from all 12 of the transit agencies we interviewed told us they measure performance in certain categories, the extent to which they measure other categories varied widely (see table 5).

Table 5. Categories Where Performance Is Measured or Studied—Transit Agency Responses

Category of performance measurement	Measures performance in category	Has studied or plans to study in ways other than performance measurement
Customer satisfaction	12	0
Ridership	12	0
On-time performance	12	0
Safety	12	0
Cost efficiency or effectiveness	11	1
Level of service	10	1
Accessibility for the elderly and persons with disabilities	10	0
Capital planning	10	1
Environmental impact and energy use	7	4
Health impact	5	3
Economic development	4	4
Connectivity between lines and modes of transportation	3	6

Source: GAO.

For example,

- Officials at all 12 transit agencies told us that they measure performance in the categories of customer satisfaction, ridership, on-time performance, and safety.
- Officials from 7 of the transit agencies told us that they measure performance in the category of environmental impact and energy use. Officials from 1 of the agencies told us that they do this by tracking greenhouse gas emissions from the agency's fuel consumption based on methodology published in an FTA report.[49] Officials at 4 other agencies said that they had studied or planned to study this category, but they do not regularly measure performance in this category.
- Officials from 4 of the transit agencies told us they measure performance in the category of economic development. According to one of these officials, to do so the agency tracks the value of property developments around transit stations. Officials from 4 other agencies told us that while their agencies do not regularly measure economic development performance, they had either periodically studied the

agency's economic impact or were planning to do so. For example, officials from 1 of these agencies said that they had studied, among other things, the direct and indirect impact of their agency's current and planned operations on the agency's local economy by tracking factors such as the agency's capital investments and procurement of goods and services. However, they do not regularly measure performance in this category.

The transit agencies we interviewed determined performance measures based on a variety of factors, including the following:

- Officials from all of the U.S. transit agencies said that federal requirements provide the basis for at least some of their performance measures. These officials added that their agencies are required to report performance data to FTA's NTD and, hence, determine certain measures of performance based on NTD requirements, as discussed earlier.
- Officials from 10 of the transit agencies said that local priorities were used to determine at least some of their performance measures. For example, officials from 1 agency said that the local metropolitan planning organization required that the agency report performance on farebox recovery, which measures the agency's recovery of its costs from fares.
- Officials from 8 of the transit agencies added that they determined some of the performance measures based on industry best practices or their agency's internal needs, such as measures used to track progress toward an agency's strategic goals.
- Officials from 4 of the U.S. transit agencies said that state reporting requirements, such as outlined in state legislation on their agency, also formed the basis for determining some of their performance measures.
- Officials from 2 of the transit agencies noted that public concerns about various issues led to the development of some performance measures. Specifically, officials from 1 agency told us that passenger concerns about their security while using the transit system led the agency to allocate more funding for its transit police force and to develop and monitor the agency's performance on a "customer security index." Officials from another said that concern about the status of a new transit development led the agency to regularly

measure and publicize performance information on the development's status.

Challenges to Measuring Performance

Transit agency officials we interviewed cited a variety of challenges associated with measuring performance. Officials from 8 of the agencies stated that measuring performance on outcomes was particularly challenging. For example, officials from 5 of these agencies told us that it is particularly challenging to determine a method for measuring economic impact or to obtain relevant data. In particular, officials from 1 agency added that measuring the agency's impact on employment generation is challenging because it is difficult to isolate the agency's effect on employment. Similarly, officials from 5 of the transit agencies said it was challenging to measure environmental impact generally because it was difficult to determine a method for measuring it or to obtain relevant data. For example, an official from 1 agency said that it is difficult to measure how much pollution a bus generates compared with the pollution from passenger vehicles that the bus is displacing, in part because emissions from these passenger vehicles can vary widely and relevant data are difficult to obtain. Moreover, we were told by officials from 7 of the transit agencies that it is challenging to measure performance because performance is affected by numerous factors that are out of a transit agency's control, like economic conditions or weather. For example, an official from 1 agency noted that ridership is affected by economic conditions, such as employment. Officials from another agency also said that ridership data can be influenced by the elimination of funding for a route because, according to the officials, the elimination of routes makes it difficult to measure annual changes in overall ridership. Additionally, officials from 1 agency told us that some transit systems operate in environments that an agency has less control over, particularly bus systems, which can make measuring performance on these systems more difficult than for dedicated systems like subways. For example, the officials said that buses, unlike subways, can travel different distances on any given day, making it difficult to measure performance on a month-to-month basis.

Performance Measurement Affects Agencies' Planning and Decision Making, but Other Factors Also Play a Role

Officials from all 12 of the transit agencies we interviewed told us that they use performance information for agency planning and decision-making purposes. Officials at 9 of the agencies said that performance information is used in decisions or planning related to funding allocations. Officials from 1 agency explained that performance-based funding allocations were critical because they help to inform the agency's annual budget process and address problems, such as deterioration of capital assets, before they can have a negative impact on the agency's performance. Officials from 2 transit agencies said that information on customer satisfaction helped them understand customer perceptions about their system, which informed decisions and planning regarding issues like funding allocations and setting of strategic goals. For example, officials from 1 of these agencies said customer perceptions about the transit system's security led the agency to make decisions and plans that included allocating more funding toward transit police, developing a customer security performance measure, and setting a strategic goal of increasing customer security. Similarly, officials from the other transit agency said that measures of customer satisfaction regarding system cleanliness led their agency to allocate funding for cleaning the system and to set a strategic goal associated with system cleanliness.

While performance affects some transit agency decisions and planning, other factors are also considered. For example:

- **Funding availability:** Officials from half of the transit agencies said that funding shortfalls made it difficult to link performance measurement to decisions and planning. For example, officials from 2 of these agencies said that the recent economic recession had reduced sales tax revenue and consequently agency funding, resulting in reduced service or plans for expansion.
- **Political priorities:** Officials from half of the transit agencies added that local political priorities also challenge the agencies' ability to link performance to decisions and planning. These officials said that among other reasons, elected officials can affect decisions and planning for routes or funding allocation based on political priorities rather than performance information.

Transit Agencies and Experts See a Role for the Federal Government in Transit, but See Challenges to Imposing National Performance Measures

Officials from the 12 transit agencies and experts from the five organizations we interviewed suggested a variety of changes to the federal role in transit:

- **Investment in existing transit infrastructure:** Officials from 3 of the transit agencies and experts from two of the organizations suggested that the federal government address the declining condition of transit agency infrastructure by focusing on state of good repair needs. Officials from 2 of these transit agencies and one of the organizations believed that federal grants for transit too often focused on new capital investments rather than updating and maintaining existing infrastructure.
- **Short duration of federal grant funding:** Officials from 3 of the transit agencies stated that the duration of federal transit programs' grant funding made it difficult for them to conduct long-term strategic planning. According to officials from 2 of these agencies, this long-term planning would benefit if grants were provided for 3- to 5-year periods.
- **Flexibility in implementing federal transit grants:** Some of the transit agency officials and experts we spoke with stated that the federal government should provide greater flexibility to transit agencies or local transportation planning officials to decide how federal grants should be used. Specifically, officials from 5 of the transit agencies and experts from three of the organizations told us that federal grants for transit systems should be less specific to particular modes, such as bus or rail. Officials from 2 of the transit agencies and experts from three of the organizations also told us that transit agencies or local transportation planning officials should have greater autonomy to determine which transportation solution would be most efficient for their circumstances.

Current SAFETEA-LU programs provide funding for accomplishing goals such as modernizing or improving existing transit equipment and facilities, providing capital assistance for new transit systems or expansion to existing systems, expanding access to elderly persons and persons with disabilities, and transporting low-income individuals to and from jobs. During interviews, experts from four of the organizations and officials from 7 of the transit agencies told us that the federal government should set goals that reflect broader issues, such as promoting economic development or improving air quality, in part to address the differences between transit agencies' circumstances and priorities. However, officials from 3 of the agencies and experts from three of the organizations told us that the goals should address transit-specific issues, such as state of good repair needs. As discussed earlier, federal transit programs focus on these issues to some extent. The transit agency officials and transit experts we interviewed offered a variety of suggestions for consideration in developing federal transit program goals, including the following:

- improve air quality;
- encourage economic growth and access to jobs;
- reduce roadway congestion;
- increase the safety of transit systems;
- provide increased mobility for populations, particularly in regions with fast-growing populations;
- encourage modal shift from automobiles to public transit; and
- promote livable communities around transit that reduces dependence on foreign oil, encourage economic growth, and addresses environmental challenges.

All of the transit agencies and expert organizations we interviewed foresaw challenges to imposing national performance accountability mechanisms on transit agencies, some of which we identified earlier in our review. Officials from 10 of the agencies and experts from three of the organizations told us that it would be challenging to account for the varying priorities of transit agencies, such as differences in the size or the density of the population they serve, or the ways in which they measure performance. For example, officials from 4 of the agencies noted a lack of consistency in how performance is measured, which makes it difficult to compare agencies' performance. The agency officials and transit experts cited a variety of other challenges that they said should be considered when implementing a more performance-based federal transit system, including the following:

- Some transit agencies, particularly in small cities or rural areas, lack personnel or technical resources to measure performance.

- Some federal support should be based on need rather than performance because of factors that could make it difficult for some agencies to meet performance goals or maintain performance standards. For example, officials from 1 of the transit agencies said that if the federal support was based on performance alone, then areas with smaller populations would not be positioned as well as agencies in larger, more populated areas to perform on measures like passengers per mile or recovery of costs from fares. Experts from one organization added that some funding for transit agencies should be allocated if there is a risk of decreased performance in the future in areas such as safety.
- For some categories of performance, like economic development, data are more difficult to obtain or performance is more difficult to measure.
- Goals attached to a federal performance mechanism could outweigh the transit needs or priorities based on local circumstances.
- Some of the transit agencies and experts we interviewed provided suggestions for implementing federal performance accountability mechanisms that would mitigate some of the challenges they discussed. For example,
- Officials from 1 transit agency suggested that a voluntary pilot program be implemented to test a rating system that would measure participating agencies' median performance over several years on a series of performance indicators. They said such a system would allow the federal government to assess how each agency is performing over time, rather than comparing agencies with differing circumstances or evaluating agencies based on a single performance measure.
- An official from 1 transit agency suggested that the federal government support the development of a national transit benchmarking system in which transit agencies could learn best practices from other agencies to improve their performance, rather than applying national performance targets that would have to account for the many differences among transit agencies. The official cited an established benchmarking system in which transit agencies can confidentially share their performance information and compare it against that of other agencies in similar groups, including large subway systems, medium subway systems, and bus systems.

- Experts from two of the organizations also told us that the federal government should offer capacity development opportunities such as technical assistance to address the lack of resources or potential burden that some transit agencies could experience with additional federal requirements for performance measurement.

Conclusion

In our 2008 report on surface transportation, we recommended that Congress consider instituting processes to make grantees more accountable by establishing more performance-based links between funding and program outcomes.[50] Implementing links between transit funding and performance through the use of financial performance accountability mechanisms and other tools and approaches, as outlined in this report, could help create incentives to local transit agencies to improve their performance. Although we have identified challenges to making the federal transit program more performance based, we have also identified ways to mitigate those challenges—through the use of strategies for implementing performance accountability mechanisms. As we have illustrated through examples and through the concerns and suggestions of local transit agency and expert officials, performance accountability mechanisms are not one-size-fits-all. Nevertheless, with careful consideration, the mechanisms and strategies highlighted in this report can be combined to achieve a more accountable federal transit program and thus lead to improved outcomes in transit and achievement of federal goals.

One FTA program, New Starts, is frequently cited as a model for other federal transportation programs, because of its use of a rigorous and systematic evaluation process to distinguish among proposed investments based on projected performance. Other FTA programs have afforded limited performance accountability, and thus little incentive to ensure federal transit grants are being used effectively and efficiently. Because of the lack of incentives of sufficient value to grantees in formula programs, the federal transit grant system has limited ability to influence the activities and priorities of local grantees and to ensure that the goals and priorities of the federal transit program are achieved. Further decreasing the federal government's ability to positively affect the performance of local transit agencies is FTA's limited analysis of the extent to which transit grants, current formula incentives, and FTA program activities have had an effect on transit agency performance. The Government Performance and Results Act of 1993, as amended, emphasized managing results and identifying opportunities to improve performance and increase accountability.[51] By not fully measuring and analyzing the effects of transit grant programs and FTA program activities on local transit agency performance, FTA is missing a valuable opportunity to assess both its own activities and the transit grant programs for needed changes.

As Congress and DOT prepare for the upcoming surface transportation reauthorization, which includes the reauthorization of all federal transit programs, the department and FTA have an opportunity to enhance the performance of transit grant programs by incorporating performance accountability mechanisms into those programs' legislative requirements. Doing so could increase the federal government's ability to ensure that federal transit grants are used efficiently and effectively and achieve the goals established by Congress, keeping in mind the challenges and strategies for mitigating those challenges that we have identified. Since little is currently known about applying these mechanisms to the transit sector, FTA could help fill that knowledge gap by analyzing the feasibility and potential impacts of options for using such mechanisms in federal transit programs and report that information to Congress to help inform the congressional deliberations on the ongoing surface transportation reauthorization.

RECOMMENDATIONS FOR EXECUTIVE ACTION

To enhance the performance of federal transit programs, we recommend that the Secretary of Transportation direct the FTA Administrator to study and report to Congress on options for adding performance accountability mechanisms to transit grant programs. FTA should strive to provide such information in time to be considered during the reauthorization of the federal transit programs.

To improve FTA's ability to determine the extent to which transit grants, current formula incentives, and FTA program activities have had a positive effect on local transit agency performance—and to the extent that FTA finds current data sources to be appropriate and reliable for such purposes—we recommend that the Secretary of Transportation direct the FTA Administrator to further analyze and use data submitted to FTA by local transit agencies. As part of this analysis, FTA may want to identify and evaluate, when applicable,

- the extent to which transit grant programs are accomplishing their established goals,

- the areas of performance in which FTA should concentrate its program activities to increase the performance of local transit agencies and the federal transit program in general, and
- the extent to which formula incentives and other performance accountability mechanisms have influenced the activities and performance of local transit agencies.

AGENCY COMMENTS AND OUR EVALUATION

We provided a draft of this report to DOT for review and comment. DOT officials provided technical clarifications, which we incorporated into the report as appropriate, and DOT said it would consider our recommendations.

David J. Wise
Director, Physical Infrastructure Issues

APPENDIX I: SCOPE AND METHODOLOGY

To address the first objective, on the extent to which federal transit programs incorporate performance in funding distribution and evaluating transit program effectiveness, we selected and reviewed 8 of 18 federal transit programs that account for nearly 97 percent of all Federal Transit Administration (FTA) grant funds, excluding funds provided under the American Recovery and Reinvestment Act.[1] With respect to the distribution of transit funds in these programs, we analyzed legislation and FTA documents and interviewed FTA officials to determine the current factors used to establish the level of grant funding under each of the transit programs and the extent, if any, to which the funding is linked to performance. In assessing the extent to which programs are funded based on performance, we compared the factors used to allocate funding to the programs against a definition of performance measures, which requires the measurement of activities against capacity, demand, or costs. To simulate incentive tier apportionments for the Urbanized Area Formula Grant Program's bus tier, we analyzed FTA apportionment documents and National Transit Database (NTD) data. Concerning the extent to which performance information is incorporated into efforts to evaluate the effectiveness of transit programs, we also analyzed FTA documents and interviewed FTA officials. We relied on criteria found in the Government Performance and Results Act, Transportation Research Board reports, and other sources, which indicate, among other things, that performance-based systems should have defined goals and objectives, link performance measures and program activities, have steps to monitor and report on performance, integrate performance results into decision making, and review and update performance systems periodically. We did not assess NTD or other FTA data to determine its reliability or appropriateness for use in assessing the performance of the Safe, Accountable, Flexible, Efficient Transportation Equity Act: A Legacy for Users (SAFETEA-LU) transit programs.

To address the second objective, on mechanisms that exist for making federal transit programs more performance based and strategies for supporting their successful implementation, we conducted a literature review to identify pertinent studies and reports and interviewed transit agency officials and industry experts. We selected studies and reports that focused on performance accountability mechanisms and general practices that facilitated the effective use of accountability mechanisms or provided examples of using performance accountability mechanisms. Our literature search covered studies published from 2004 onward and was largely drawn from major electronic databases in transportation, economics, and other fields (e.g., Transportation Research Information Services, EconLit, ProQuest, WorldCat, and other databases) and from our past work in surface transportation and performance measures and management. We also interviewed transit agency officials (see list of agencies in table 6) and a variety of industry experts to obtain their views on performance accountability mechanisms, their advantages and disadvantages, and strategies for mitigating any disadvantages and for helping support their successful implementation. We identified industry experts through a literature review and interviews with officials from FTA. Collectively, these experts were knowledgeable about the transit issues that we were addressing.[2] In addition to the literature review, the examples of agencies or programs where the mechanisms have been proposed for or actually used were identified from other sources, including our previous work and interviews with transit agency officials and experts.

To address the third objective, describing how selected U.S. and foreign transit agencies incorporate performance measurement into their planning and decision making and their views on the federal role in transit, we conducted semistructured interviews with 12 transit agencies—10 from the United States and 2 from foreign countries (see table 6). We identified transit agencies for our analysis through a literature review and interviews with officials from FTA and industry organizations. We further narrowed the list by reviewing the transit agencies' Web sites for information about their use of performance measurement to ensure the transit agency would be able to discuss performance measurement. The 10 U.S. agencies were selected to ensure geographic distribution and variation in the size of the population served. To select the 2 foreign transit agencies for our review, we narrowed the list to include agencies that offer multiple modes of transit and that were available to speak with us in English. Because the agencies were selected as a nonprobability sample, the results cannot be generalized to all transit agencies.[3] However, the information from these agencies is illustrative of the ways in which transit agencies can incorporate performance measurement into their planning and decision-making processes. We also conducted interviews with industry experts, as previously discussed, to obtain their views on the role of the federal government in transit.

Table 6. Transit Agencies Interviewed for GAO's Analysis

Agency location: state or country	Major area(s) served	Transit agency name
California	San Francisco	Bay Area Rapid Transit
Canada	Montreal	Société de transport de Montréal
Colorado	Denver	Regional Transportation District
Illinois	Chicago	Regional Transportation Authority
Kansas	Wichita	Wichita Transit
Maryland, Virginia, Washington, D.C.	Washington	Washington Metropolitan Area Transportation Authority
Oregon	Portland	Tri-County Metropolitan Transportation District of Oregon
Pennsylvania	Philadelphia	Southeastern Pennsylvania Transportation Authority
Texas	Dallas	Dallas Area Rapid Transit
United Kingdom	London	Transport for London
Utah	Salt Lake City	Utah Transit Authority
Virginia	Norfolk and Virginia Beach	Hampton Roads Transit

Source: GAO.

We conducted this performance audit from November 2009 through November 2010 in accordance with generally accepted government auditing standards. Those standards require that we plan and perform the audit to obtain sufficient, appropriate evidence to provide a reasonable basis for our findings and conclusions based on our audit objectives. We believe that the evidence obtained provides a reasonable basis for our findings and conclusions based on our audit objectives.

End Notes

[1] American Public Transportation Association, *Impacts of the Recession on Public Transportation Agencies, Survey Results* (Washington, D.C.: March 2010).

[2] GAO, *Surface Transportation: Restructured Federal Approach Needed for More Focused, Performance-Based, and Sustainable Programs*, GAO-08-400 (Washington, D.C.: Mar. 6, 2008), and *Performance and Accountability: Transportation Challenges Facing Congress and the Department of Transportation*, GAO-07-545T (Washington, D.C.: Mar. 6, 2007).

[3] SAFETEA-LU, Pub. L. No. 109-59, 119 Stat. 1144 (Aug. 10, 2005).

[4] SAFETEA-LU expired at the end of fiscal year 2009. Since that time, Congress has enacted the Surface Transportation Extension Act of 2010, title IV of Pub. L. No. 111-147, 124 Stat. 71 (March 18, 2010), which continues the authorization of the federal transit programs through December 31, 2010. Additionally, the Consolidated Appropriations Act, 2010, div. A, title I of Pub. L. No. 111-117, 123 Stat. 3034 (Dec. 16, 2009), appropriated funds for Federal Transit Administration funded programs for fiscal year 2010.

[5] Pub. L. No. 111-5, 123 Stat. 115 (Feb. 17, 2009).

[6] Government Performance and Results Act of 1993, Pub. L. No. 103-62, 107 Stat. 285 (Aug. 3, 1993).

[7] An urbanized area is an area with a population of 50,000 or more that is designated as such in the 2000 Census by the U.S. Department of Commerce, Bureau of the Census.

[8] Designated recipients are entities designated by the chief executive officer of a state, responsible local officials, and publicly owned operators of public transportation to receive and apportion amounts that are attributable to transportation management areas. 49 U.S.C. § 5307(a)(2). The designated recipient is responsible, among other things, for allocating annual apportionments among recipients in an urbanized area or areas based on local needs and arrangements, and in coordination with the MPO, submitting a grant application for the Section 5307 Program of Projects, and/or designating other eligible applicants to apply for all or part of the apportionments, and notifying FTA of such designations. FTA C 9030 1D, *Urbanized Area Formula Program Guidance and Application Instructions*, Chapter II-3, section 5(a) and (c) (Washington D.C.: May 1, 2010).

[9] 49 U.S.C. § 5307.

[10] 49 U.S.C. § 5311.

[11] Fixed-guideway systems use and occupy a separate right-of-way for the exclusive use of public transportation services. They include fixed rail, exclusive lanes for buses, and other systems. See 49 U.S.C. § 5302 (4).

[12] 49 U.S.C. § 5309.

[13] 49 U.S.C. § 5309, 49 U.S.C. § 5318.

[14] 49 U.S.C. § 5309.

[15] 42 U.S.C. §12101 *et seq.*

[16] The designated recipient or state will apply to FTA for funding on behalf of itself and any subrecipients within its area.

[17] 49 U.S.C. § 5317.

[18] The designated recipient or state will apply to FTA for funding on behalf of itself and any subrecipients within its area.

[19] 49 U.S.C. § 5316.

[20] Local governmental authorities may be grant recipients when Federal Highway Administration funds are flexed to Section 5310 support services for individuals with disabilities.

[21] A state may allocate amounts to a private nonprofit organization if the public transportation service is unavailable, insufficient, or inappropriate. 49 U.S.C. § 5310(a)(2)(A). A state may allocate funds to a governmental authority that is approved by the state or certifies that there are not any nonprofit organizations readily available in the area to provide the services. 49 U.S.C. § 5310(a)(2)(B).

[22] 49 U.S.C. § 5310.

[23] American Public Transportation Association, *Impacts of the Recession on Public Transportation Agencies: Survey Results* (Washington, D.C.: March 2010).

[24] Paratransit services are transportation services that are typically provided to targeted populations, such as the elderly or those with disabilities, without fixed routes or timetables. See 42 U.S.C. § 12143.

[25] The grant life cycle includes the application, award, and closeout phases.

[26] GAO, *Public Transportation: Improvements are Needed to More Fully Assess Predicted Impacts of New Starts Projects*, GAO-08-844 (Washington, D.C.: July 25, 2008).

[27] See 49 U.S.C. § 5336.

[28] Under the Small Transit Intensive Cities (STIC) Program, additional funding is apportioned to urbanized areas with populations of fewer than 200,000 that meet or exceed, in one or more of six performance categories, the industry average for all urbanized areas with a population of at least 200,000 but not more than 999,999. The measures for this program include vehicle revenue miles per capita and passenger miles per vehicle revenue mile. 49 U.S.C. § 5336(i)(1) and (j).

[29] A vehicle revenue mile is the distance traveled by a transit vehicle between the time it is first available to the public and the last passenger drop-off.

[30] Funding for urbanized areas with populations above 200,000 under the Urbanized Areas Formula Program is apportioned and flows directly to a designated recipient for the urbanized area and is then divided among eligible transit agencies within the urbanized area. 49 U.S.C. § 5307(a)(2).

[31] Department of Transportation, *FY2009 Performance & Accountability Report (Washington, D.C: November 16, 2009).*

[32] The Americans with Disabilities Act (ADA) of 1990 requires that transit operators provide accessible paratransit service that is comparable to their regular service for disabled individuals who are unable to provide their own transportation or access the regular transit system. See 42 U.S.C. § 12143.

[33] See 49 U.S.C. § 5335 for reporting requirements under the NTD. Transit agencies that receive federal funding under specific programs (Urbanized Area Formula Grants and Nonurbanized Area Formula Grants) are required to submit data to the NTD, 49 U.S.C. § 5335(b).

[34] We have not analyzed the reliability or completeness of NTD or other data collected by FTA for the purposes of assessing transit agency performance or awarding grant funding based on transit agency performance.

[35] Under GPRA, FTA is required to establish performance goals to define the level of performance to be achieved and to establish performance indicators to be used in measuring or assessing the relevant outputs, service levels, and outcomes for each of its program activities. 31 U.S.C. § 1115.

[36] FTA C 9070.1F, *Elderly Individuals and Individuals with Disabilities Program Guidance and Application Instructions,* Chapter II, Section 3 (a) and (b), (Washington, D.C.: May 1, 2007).

[37] FTA C 9050.1, *The Job Access and Reverse Commute (JARC) Program Guidance and Application Instructions,* Chapter II, Section 3 (a) and (b) (Washington, D.C.: May 1, 2007).

[38] FTA C 9045.1, *New Freedom Program Guidance and Application Instructions,* Chapter II, Section 3 (a) and (b) (Washington, D.C.: May 1, 2007).

[39] GAO, *Managing for Results: Enhancing Agency Use of Performance Information for Management Decision Making,* GAO-05-927 (Washington, D.C.: Sept. 9, 2005).

[40] U.S. Department of Transportation, FHWA and FTA, *2008 Status of the Nation's Highways, Bridges, and Transit: Conditions and Performance Report to Congress.*

[41] Cook, Thomas J., and Judwon Lawrie, *Use of Performance Standards and Measures for Public Transportation Systems,* Institute for Transportation Research and Education, North Carolina State University, Final Report FHWA/NC/2004-10 (Raleigh, North Carolina: September 2004).

[42] Cook, Thomas J., and Judwon Lawrie, Final Report FHWA/NC/2004-10 (2004).

[43] All of the FTA grants programs we reviewed require that grantees provide sufficient funds or approved in-kind resources to serve as a local match for federally assisted projects. For example, the Job Access and Reverse Commute Program requires that the local share of eligible capital and planning costs be no less than 20 percent of the net program costs and the local share for eligible operating costs be no less than 50 percent of net operating costs.

[44] Transit Cooperative Research Program (TCRP), Synthesis 56, *Performance-Based Measures in Transit Fund Allocation: A Synthesis of Transit Practice*, (Washington, D.C.: 2004).

[45] GAO, *Vocational Rehabilitation Funding Formula: Options for Improving Equity in State Grants and Considerations for Performance Incentives,* GAO-09-798 (Washington D.C.: Sept. 30, 2009).

[46] GAO, *Grants Management: Enhancing Performance Accountability Provisions Could Lead to Better Results,* GAO-06-1046 (Washington D.C.: Sept. 29, 2006).

[47] GAO-06-1046.

[48] GAO-06-1046.

[49] Federal Transit Administration, *Public Transportation's Role in Responding to Climate Change.* (Washington, D.C.: January 2010).

[50] GAO, *Surface Transportation: Restructured Federal Approach Needed for More Focused, Performance-Based, and Sustainable Programs*, GAO-08-400 (Washington, D.C.: Mar. 6, 2008).

[51] GAO, *The Government Performance and Results Act: 1997 Governmentwide Implementation Will Be Uneven,* GAO/GGD-97-109 (Washington, D.C.: June 2, 1997).

End Notes for Appendix I

[1] The 8 programs include New Starts, the Bus and Bus Related Equipment and Facilities Program, Fixed-Guideway Modernization, the Urbanized Area Formula Program, the

Nonurbanized Area Formula Program, the Special Needs of Elderly Individuals and Individuals with Disabilities Program, the Job Access and Reverse Commute Program, and the New Freedom Program.

[2] The experts were from a variety of organizations including the American Public Transportation Association, the Bipartisan Policy Center, Transportation for America/Reconnecting America, the Railway Transport and Strategy Center at Imperial College of London (benchmarking programs), the Transit Finance Learning Exchange, and the Metropolitan Washington Council of Governments.

[3] Results from nonprobability samples cannot be used to make inferences about a population because in a nonprobability sample, some elements of the population being studied have no chance or an unknown chance of being selected as part of the sample.

In: Performance-Based Transportation Programs ISBN: 978-1-63482-722-5
Editor: Travis Schmidt

Chapter 3

STATEWIDE TRANSPORTATION PLANNING: OPPORTUNITIES EXIST TO TRANSITION TO PERFORMANCE-BASED PLANNING AND FEDERAL OVERSIGHT*

United States Government Accountability Office

WHY GAO DID THIS STUDY

Through the statewide transportation planning process, states decide how to spend federal transportation funds—almost $46 billion in fiscal year 2009. Draft legislation to reauthorize federal surface transportation legislation would, among other things, revise planning requirements to recognize states' use of rural planning organizations (RPO) and require performance measurement. As requested, GAO examined (1) states' planning activities and RPOs' satisfaction that rural needs are considered, (2) states' planning challenges, (3) the U.S. Department of Transportation's (USDOT) approach to overseeing statewide planning, and (4) states' use of performance measurement and opportunities to make statewide planning more performance based. GAO analyzed planning documents; surveyed departments of transportation in 50 states, Puerto Rico, and Washington, D.C., and 569 RPOs;

---

* This is an edited, reformatted and augmented version of a U.S. Government Accountability Office report, GAO-11-77, dated December 2010.

interviewed officials in 6 states; and held an expert panel on performance-based planning.

WHAT GAO RECOMMENDS

To make statewide planning more performance based, Congress should consider requiring states to update their long-range plans on a prescribed schedule, identifying outcomes for statewide planning and directing USDOT to assess states' progress in achieving them, and requiring USDOT and states to collaboratively develop performance measures. USDOT provided technical comments which we incorporated into the report as appropriate.

WHAT GAO FOUND

States conduct a variety of long- and short-range planning activities, and the majority of RPOs surveyed reported being generally satisfied that rural needs are considered. To develop required long-range statewide transportation plans (long-range plans), states conduct research activities, such as inventorying assets and modeling traffic. While the resulting plans generally include some performance elements, such as goals, many plans do not include performance targets. Such targets are not required, but prior GAO work shows that targets are useful tools to indicate progress toward achieving goals. To develop required short-range plans—state transportation improvement programs (STIP)—states assess needs and determine funding allocations. However, in selecting projects, states assigned greater importance to factors such as political and public support than to economic analysis of project benefits and costs. While the majority of surveyed RPOs reported being satisfied that their rural needs were considered, some RPOs reported less satisfaction with their role in allocating funds for rural areas.

States commonly cited insufficient or uncertain funding to implement transportation projects among the primary challenges to long- and short-range planning. States also reported that involving the public and addressing transportation data limitations were significant long-range planning challenges. Short-range planning challenges included meeting federal requirements to demonstrate the availability of sufficient project funding and to update the STIP to reflect changes.

USDOT has a limited role in the oversight of long-range plans, and pursuant to federal law, its STIP oversight focuses on states' compliance with procedures. Furthermore, USDOT is not required to review long-range plans, states are not required to update them on a schedule, and some states reported infrequent updates. For example, 10 states reported not updating plans since the most recent surface transportation authorization in 2005. Limited USDOT oversight and infrequent updates present risks, including the ineffective use of federal planning funds. For the STIP, USDOT's oversight focuses, as required, on states' compliance with federal planning procedures. Information on whether states achieve outcomes such as reducing congestion is limited.

While states are not required to set performance outcomes in planning, most states reported using performance measurement in the areas of safety and asset condition. Several challenges limit broader use of performance measures, including identifying indicators for qualitative measures such as livability and collecting data across transportation modes. Through our expert panel and interviews, we identified several elements that could improve states' use of performance measures, including national goals, federal and state collaboration on developing performance measures, appropriate targets, and revised federal oversight focusing on monitoring states' progress in meeting outcomes.

ABBREVIATIONS

AASHTO	American Association of State Highway Transportation Officials
FHWA	Federal Highway Administration
FTA	Federal Transit Administration
GHSA	Governors Highway Safety Association
GPRA	Government Performance and Results Act of 1993
HPMS	Highway Performance Monitoring System
MDOT	Montana Department of Transportation
MPO	metropolitan planning organization
NHTSA	National Highway Traffic Safety Administration
PennDOT	Pennsylvania Department of Transportation
RPO	rural planning organization
SAFETEA-LU	Safe, Accountable, Flexible, Efficient Transportation Equity Act: A Legacy for Users
state DOT	state departments of transportation
STIP	state transportation improvement program

SPR	FHWA's State Planning and Research Program
SPRP	FTA's State Planning and Research Program
TIP	transportation improvement program
TIGER	Transportation Investment Generating Economic Recovery
USDOT	U.S. Department of Transportation

View GAO-11-77 Key Component

Statewide Transportation Planning: Surveys of State Departments of Transportation and Regional Planning and Development Organizations (GAO-11-78SP), an e-supplement to GAO-11-77

* * *

December 15, 2010

The Honorable James L. Oberstar
Chairman
Committee on Transportation and Infrastructure
House of Representatives

Dear Mr. Chairman:

The statewide transportation planning process, administered through each state's department of transportation (state DOT), is the forum through which states decide how to spend significant amounts of federal surface transportation funds. In fiscal year 2009, the U.S. Department of Transportation (USDOT) apportioned almost $46 billion to states and urbanized areas for highway and transit projects to be developed through the statewide transportation planning process. This amount included almost $36 billion for highway infrastructure projects through the Federal Highway Administration (FHWA) and approximately $10 billion in transit grants to urbanized areas and states through the Federal Transit Administration (FTA). The statewide transportation planning process is informed by transportation planning performed by metropolitan planning organizations (MPO) that lead transportation planning in urbanized areas—geographic areas with a population of 50,000 or more. Although states must comply with federal planning requirements administered jointly by FHWA and FTA, states have considerable discretion to allocate federal funds and select projects. We recently reported that in fiscal years 2007 and 2008, all states received more federal funding for highway programs than users contributed to the Highway Account of the Highway Trust Fund, the primary source of federal highway and transit funds.[1] At the same time, estimates of the costs to repair or upgrade aging transportation infrastructure—as well as expand capacity to meet increased demand—top hundreds of billions of dollars. Hence, decisions made in the statewide transportation planning process are critical to ensuring that limited federal transportation funds are spent wisely and deliver intended results.

Funding for federal surface transportation programs, including statewide transportation planning, is authorized under the Safe, Accountable, Flexible, Efficient Transportation Equity Act: A Legacy for Users (SAFETEA-LU), which expired in September 2009. The Surface Transportation Extension Act of 2010 extended the funding authorization for SAFETEA-LU programs through December 31, 2010.[2] Congress is currently developing legislation for a new surface transportation authorization. In recent years, we have asked Congress to consider refocusing surface transportation programs to make them more performance based.[3] In 2009, the House Committee on Transportation and Infrastructure issued draft legislation to reauthorize surface transportation programs that proposes moving statewide transportation planning toward a more performance-based framework.[4] The draft legislation would also recognize state-designated rural planning organizations (RPO)—planning bodies representing areas with a population of less than 50,000 people—and direct states to coordinate with such organizations in the statewide transportation planning process. To help inform congressional efforts, you asked us to provide information on current statewide transportation planning activities, challenges, and oversight. Accordingly, we examined

- planning activities conducted by state DOTs and the extent to which RPOs are satisfied that rural needs are considered in statewide planning,
- challenges encountered by state DOTs in carrying out planning responsibilities,
- FHWA's and FTA's approach to overseeing statewide transportation planning, and

- the extent to which state DOTs are using performance measurement for planning and opportunities to make statewide planning more performance based.

To gather information for addressing all these issues, we reviewed and analyzed federal and state planning documents and applicable laws and regulations, and surveyed state DOTs in all 50 states, the District of Columbia, and Puerto Rico, receiving responses from 100 percent of those surveyed.[5] We also interviewed federal, state, and local planning officials in Louisiana, Montana, Pennsylvania, Texas, Washington state, and West Virginia. These states were selected to obtain a diverse mix of planning contexts based on geography, percentage of the population covered by MPOs, and stakeholder recommendations, among other factors. To determine the extent to which RPOs are satisfied that rural needs are considered in statewide planning, we surveyed 569 regional planning and development organizations in the 50 states to identify those organizations that coordinate or conduct surface transportation planning in nonmetropolitan areas, referred to as RPOs in this report.[6] We received responses from 409 organizations, or 72 percent of those surveyed. To describe FHWA's and FTA's approach to overseeing statewide transportation planning, we reviewed FHWA and FTA documents and interviewed officials at USDOT headquarters, six FHWA division offices, and four FTA regional offices. To identify opportunities to make statewide planning more performance based, we convened a panel of transportation planning experts through the National Academy of Sciences, and we interviewed transportation planning stakeholders.

We conducted this performance audit from October 2009 through December 2010 in accordance with generally accepted government auditing standards. Those standards require that we plan and perform the audit to obtain sufficient, appropriate evidence to provide a reasonable basis for our findings and conclusions based on our audit objectives. We believe that the evidence obtained provides a reasonable basis for our findings and conclusions based on our audit objectives. See appendix I for more detailed information on our scope and methodology and appendix II for additional information on the results of our RPO survey. In addition, see the electronic supplement to this report—GAO-11-78SP—for a complete list of frequencies for questions from both surveys.

We provided a copy of this report to USDOT for review and comment. USDOT officials provided technical comments which we incorporated into the report, as appropriate.

BACKGROUND

Each state, as well as the District of Columbia and Puerto Rico, is required to carry out a continuing, cooperative, and comprehensive statewide transportation planning process. The statewide transportation planning process addresses both urbanized and nonmetropolitan areas of the state and includes both highway and transit needs. For urbanized areas with a population of 50,000 or more, state DOTs must coordinate planning activities with MPOs—federally recognized and funded organizations representing local governments that lead transportation planning activities in metropolitan areas. To receive federal transportation funding, any project in an urbanized area must emerge from the relevant MPO and state DOT planning process. For nonmetropolitan areas not covered by an MPO, states must consult with and provide opportunities for local officials to participate in statewide planning. Some states choose to fulfill this requirement by consulting with RPOs, which are typically voluntary planning organizations that serve as a forum for local officials to develop consensus on regional transportation priorities. In some cases, RPOs may serve a wide geographic area comprising multiple rural counties whose combined population may greatly exceed 50,000. States without RPOs may consult directly with nonmetropolitan local officials with responsibility for transportation planning to fulfill their consultation requirements.

To meet federal planning requirements, states must develop a long-range statewide transportation plan[7] and a state transportation improvement program (STIP) (see figure 1). The long-range statewide transportation plan establishes a state's strategic vision and direction for its transportation investments for at least a 20-year period. This plan may vary in content from state to state, from a broad, policy-oriented document to a document containing specific project information. However, the plan must provide for the development and implementation of a multimodal transportation system for all areas of the state, and for public comment before it is published. Currently, there are no requirements for the long-range statewide transportation plan to include specific project information, a financial plan demonstrating how the plan is to be funded and implemented, performance measures for achieving goals, or a regularly updated schedule, and the state is not required to obtain federal approval for the plan. The STIP is the state program of transportation projects covering at least a 4-year period that are to be supported with federal surface transportation funds, as well as regionally significant projects requiring an action by FHWA or FTA, whether or not federally funded. Each project must be consistent with the long-range statewide transportation plan and approved long-range metropolitan transportation plans. The STIP must be fiscally constrained, meaning it shall include a project, or an identified phase of a project, only if full funding can reasonably be anticipated within the time period contemplated for completion of the project. Although federal planning statutes and regulations do not define specific national goals or outcomes that states should address in their planning documents, the statewide planning process must provide for the consideration and implementation of specific statutorily defined planning factors in developing both the long-range statewide transportation plan and the STIP, which include economic vitality, safety and security, accessibility and mobility, protecting and enhancing the environment, and promoting energy conservation, among others.[8]

MPOs are also required to produce a long-range transportation plan, referred to as a metropolitan transportation plan, and a transportation improvement program (TIP). The metropolitan transportation plan spans at least 20 years and includes long- and short-range strategies and actions to ensure an effective, integrated multimodal transportation system. The TIP spans at least 4 years and includes all projects in the MPO's jurisdiction that are to receive federal surface transportation funding or that are of regional significance. The TIP must, at a minimum, be updated every 4 years, and the metropolitan transportation plan must be updated every 4 or 5 years.[9] Both the TIP and the metropolitan transportation plan must be fiscally constrained. In addition, MPOs serving urbanized areas with a population of more than 200,000 are required to develop a congestion management process that identifies actions and strategies to reduce congestion. States participate in the metropolitan planning process by, for example, reviewing and approving the MPO's TIP. If the state approves the TIP, the state must incorporate it, without change, into the STIP.

At least every 4 years, state DOTs are required to submit an updated STIP to FHWA and FTA for review and approval, in which the state certifies that the transportation planning process has been carried out in accordance with federal planning requirements. FHWA and FTA must review each state DOT's STIP and make a joint finding on the extent to which the STIP is based on a planning process that meets or substantially meets the federal planning requirements, including but not limited to whether the state has demonstrated fiscal constraint in the STIP, used a documented process for involving the public and consulting with nonmetropolitan local officials, and included MPO TIP projects in the STIP. USDOT is not required to review or approve long-range statewide transportation plans, but states must provide copies of any new or amended plans to USDOT for informational purposes.[10]

The Federal-Aid Highway Program is administered through a federal-state partnership. State and local governments execute the programs by matching and distributing federal funds; planning, selecting, and supervising projects; and complying with federal requirements. FHWA, through its division office in each state, delivers technical expertise and fulfills oversight functions. Federal transit programs are generally administered through a federal-local partnership, although rural programs are administered at the state level. FTA, through its headquarters and 10 regional offices, provides financial assistance, establishes requirements, performs oversight, and conducts research. Grant recipients such as local transit agencies are responsible for matching federal funds and for planning, selecting, and executing projects while complying with federal requirements.

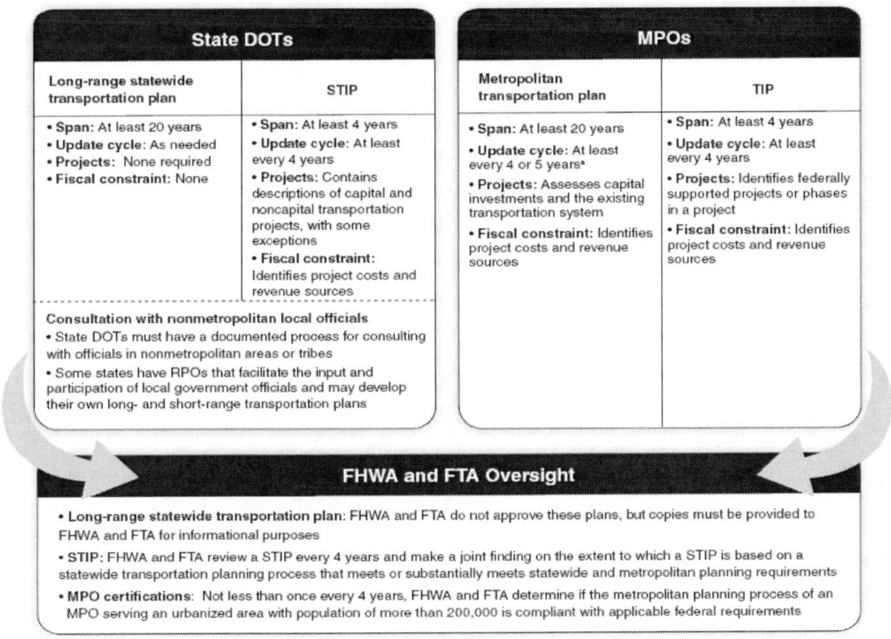

Sources: GAO analysis of federal planning requirements and FHWA and FTA documents.

[a]MPOs are required to review and update the transportation plan at least every 4 years in air quality nonattainment and maintenance areas and at least every 5 years in attainment areas.

Figure 1. Statewide Transportation Planning Roles and Responsibilities.

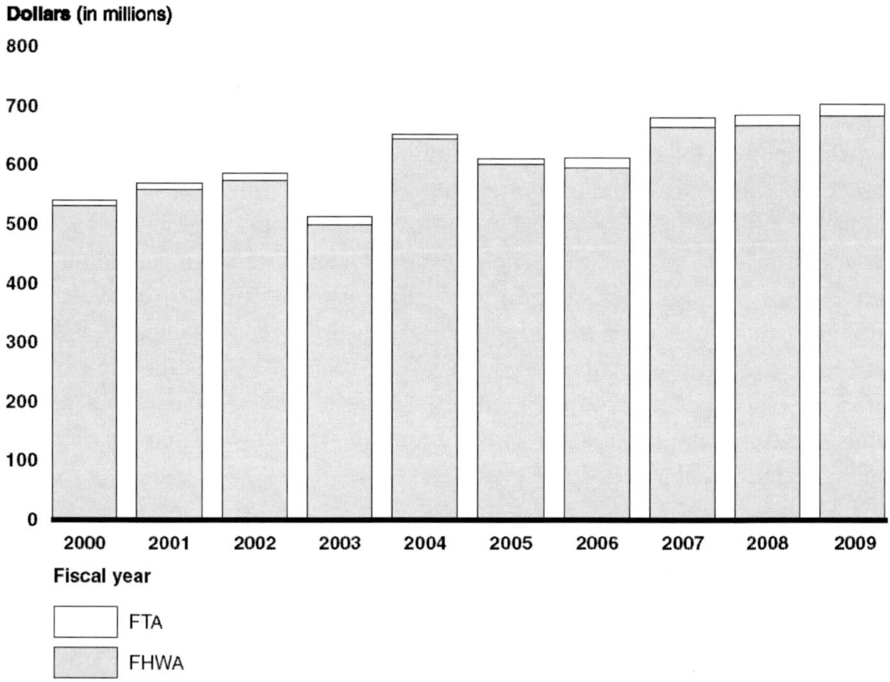

Source: FHWA and FTA notices.

Note: The FHWA planning funds depicted here are SPR program funds authorized under 23 U.S.C. § 505, and the FTA planning funds are SPRP funds authorized under 49 U.S.C. § 5305.

Figure 2. Total State Apportionments of FHWA and FTA Statewide Transportation Planning Funds, Fiscal Years 2000 through 2009.

In supporting the statewide transportation planning process, FHWA provides states with the bulk of the federal funding for planning and research (see figure 2). Through its State Planning and Research (SPR) program, FHWA provides sums equal to 2 percent of each state's formula apportionment for several Federal-Aid Highway programs.[11] In fiscal year 2009, FHWA provided states with a total of more than $680 million in SPR funds. FHWA regulations give states significant flexibility in applying SPR funds for planning—as long as FHWA has determined that the state has collected data that FHWA requires on the performance, condition, and use of the nation's transportation systems, including the condition of road and pavement surfaces. These data are collected through FHWA's Highway Performance Monitoring System (HPMS) and they constitute some of the performance data that states collect on the condition of their public roads.[12] A state may apply up to 75 percent of its annual SPR allocation to activities of its choosing to support long- and short-range planning requirements, but generally must expend no less than 25 percent of its annual SPR funds on research, development, and technology transfer activities. State DOTs may apply their SPR funds to in-house planning activities or allocate amounts to support the planning activities of MPOs, RPOs, or other planning partners.[13] States must document activities proposed to be accomplished with SPR funds, and FHWA must approve these activities. FTA apportions planning funds to states through its State Planning and Research Program (SPRP).[14] As with their SPR funds, states may authorize some of their SPRP assistance to support the planning activities of MPOs, local governments, or other planning organizations. State DOTs are encouraged to provide FTA with an SPRP work program in their SPRP grant applications.

In recent years, we have recommended that federal transportation programs be based on well-defined goals and that planning be more performance based and better linked to outcomes. We have previously reported that, for many surface transportation programs, goals are numerous and conflicting and federal oversight of these programs has no relationship to the performance of either the transportation system or of the grantees receiving federal funds.[15] Performance measurement, a central component of performance-based planning, is the ongoing monitoring and reporting of program accomplishments. As our prior work has shown, measuring performance allows organizations to track the progress they are making toward their goals and gives managers crucial information on which to base their organizational and management decisions. Recently, we asked Congress to consider making federal and metropolitan transportation programs more performance based by requiring MPOs to identify specific transportation planning outcomes and requiring DOT to assess MPOs' progress in achieving these outcomes through a certification review process.[16] Draft legislation authorizing surface transportation programs would require USDOT to set transportation planning performance measures for MPOs and require MPOs to develop performance targets to meet those measures.[17] In addition, we have recommended that FHWA link its activities and staff expectations to its oversight goals and measures and to develop an overall plan for its oversight activities tied to goals and measures.[18]

STATE DOTS CONDUCT A VARIETY OF LONG- AND SHORT-RANGE PLANNING ACTIVITIES, AND SURVEYED RPOS ARE GENERALLY SATISFIED THEIR NEEDS ARE CONSIDERED

State DOTs Conduct Several Research Activities to Develop Long-Range Plans, but Many Plans Do Not Include Performance Elements and Project-Specific Information

Through our survey and interviews, we found that state DOTs commonly conduct several research activities in developing their long-range statewide transportation plans, including developing inventories and reviewing existing transportation assets, conducting corridor studies, and using transportation demand models. In addition, most state DOTs reported that their long-range statewide transportation plans include some performance-based planning elements, such as broad goals and objectives for the state's transportation system, but most state DOTs reported that their plans do not include other key elements, such as quantitative performance targets and project and cost information.

Long-Range Planning Research Activities

Developing inventories and reviewing existing transportation assets. Forty-six state DOTs reported that they inventoried major elements of their existing transportation system, such as interstate highways and bridges, and 34 state DOTs reported that they reviewed the condition of existing assets to determine those with the greatest need. USDOT officials and transportation stakeholders told us that many state DOTs have focused their statewide long-range planning efforts on maintaining the condition and operation of their existing assets. States must collect pavement condition and other data and annually report these data to FHWA's HPMS program, generally using SPR funds to pay for the data collection. States must also inspect and report on the condition of their bridges, generally every 2 years, through FHWA's National Bridge Inspection Program. As we previously reported, many states use bridge management systems for gathering and analyzing data on bridge conditions, such as structural adequacy and safety. These systems help states manage their bridge assets and more efficiently allocate limited resources among competing priorities.[19] For example, Pennsylvania DOT (PennDOT) and Montana DOT

(MDOT) maintain road and bridge management systems to track the condition of pavement surfaces and the structural sufficiency of bridges. MDOT reported that information generated by these systems is used to track the actual performance of the highway system after investments are implemented, to show progress in meeting long-range goals.

Conducting corridor studies. In our survey, 34 state DOTs reported conducting regional and statewide corridor studies for the statewide planning process. Through corridor studies, state DOTs can focus their research on roadways with critical importance by monitoring variables such as traffic flow and congestion, trip time, and crash and safety data. Federal planning regulations encourage states to consider strategies to address corridors where congestion threatens the efficient functioning of the state's transportation system.[20] For example, officials with Colorado DOT reported that its long-range plan is corridor-based, in that the state worked with MPOs and RPOs across the state to define a vision for each of the 350 corridor segments in the state and to establish need categories for each corridor that consider financial abilities and limitations.

Using transportation demand models. In our survey, 29 state DOTs reported using a statewide transportation demand model, also known as a travel demand model, and about half of all state DOTs reported using such models to develop scenarios to inform their long-range statewide transportation plan. Used to forecast future travel demand, the models provide planners with important information on how population growth and proposed investments could affect the operation of the transportation system. Such models, however, are complex and require extensive technical capacity and current information on roadway and transit system characteristics and operations, as well as current and projected demographic information. According to stakeholders that we interviewed, some states do not have sufficient data to produce travel demand models that can be used to forecast future transportation needs across the state. Some of the highway performance data that states collect through FHWA's HPMS program could be useful for travel demand modeling—including data on population and land area, the number of vehicle miles traveled on some public roads, and the percentage of vehicle miles traveled by various vehicle types. Officials from one MPO we interviewed reported that statewide travel demand modeling is less valuable than such modeling in MPO areas, where congestion is a greater concern. To address modeling and other technical aspects of planning, the vast majority of state DOTs (45) reported that they procured contractor services in developing their statewide long-range plans.

Long-Range Statewide Transportation Plan Elements

Nearly all state DOTs reported including broad goals and objectives in their long-range statewide transportation plans, but, according to our survey, many plans do not include quantitative performance targets and project-specific information, such as fiscally constrained financial plans, project lists, and cost estimates (see figure 3). Although federal statutes or planning regulations do not require states to include quantitative performance targets in their long-range statewide transportation plans, some states reported including them, and we have previously reported that similar targets should be included in similar strategic plans developed by federal agencies.[21] In addition, project-specific information is not required to be included in long-range statewide transportation plans, although some states provide these elements in their plans.

Broad goals and objectives. All 52 state DOTs reported including broad state transportation goals, and nearly all (50) reported including objectives in their long-range statewide transportation plans. According to USDOT, goals represent the desired outcomes for the transportation system as a whole, and objectives are specific, measurable statements that identify what is to be accomplished in order to attain the goals.[22] Such goals and objectives in long-range statewide transportation plans should lead to strategies and investments that support the attainment of objectives. Federal planning regulations do not establish specific national goals or desired outcomes for states to address in their long-range statewide transportation plans, although states must consider specific statutorily defined planning factors in their planning process.[23]

Quantitative performance targets. Fewer state DOTs (18) reported including quantitative performance targets to measure progress in achieving state transportation goals. Although quantitative performance targets are not federally required for long-range statewide transportation plans, the Government Performance and Results Act of 1993 (GPRA) requires federal agencies in their strategic plans to develop performance goals that are objective, quantifiable, and measurable, and to establish performance measures that adequately indicate progress toward achieving those goals.[24] Our guidance to federal agencies developing GPRA-required annual performance plans states that an agency's performance goals and measures usually should include a quantifiable, numerical target level or other measurable value.[25] Although not required, performance targets within long-range statewide transportation plans could provide a performance standard by which the state DOT can demonstrate to the public what effect its investment decisions are having on achieving the goals established in the plan. Similarly, 13 state DOTs reported that their long-range statewide transportation plan provides a method for the public to track progress in implementing the plan. For example, PennDOT publishes an annual implementation report that details actions for achieving plan strategies and specific responsibilities and time lines for implementing the plan.

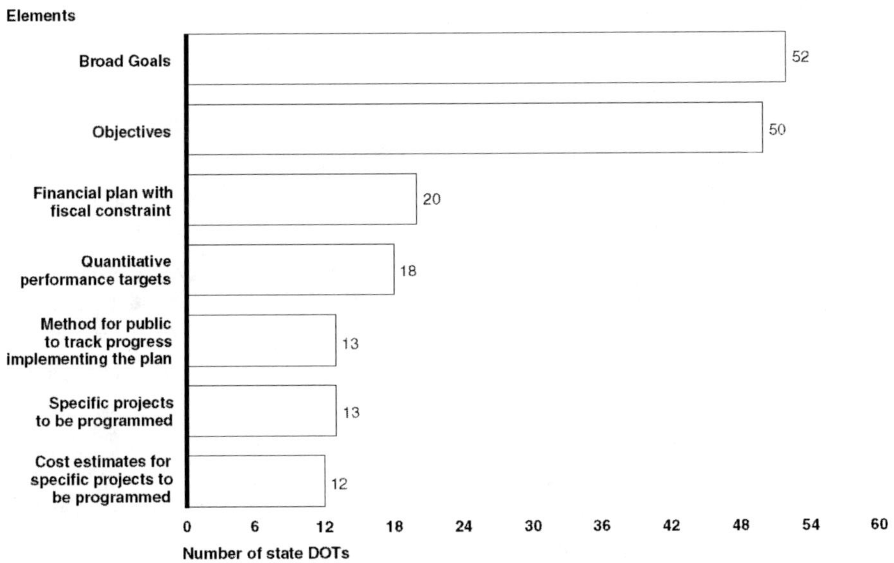

Source: State DOT survey.

Note: State DOTs also indicated that their long-range statewide transportation plans provided additional elements that were not included in this figure. For example, 36 state DOTs reported that their long-range statewide transportation plans included a statewide freight transportation strategy, 34 state DOTs reported that their long-range statewide transportation plans included a statewide intermodal transportation strategy, and 23 state DOTs reported that their long-range statewide transportation plans identified regionally significant projects. See the e-supplement—GAO-11-78SP—for additional information.

Figure 3. Selected Elements State DOTs Reported Including in Their Long-Range Statewide Transportation Plans.

Project-specific elements. The majority of state DOTs reported that their long-range plans did not include project-specific information, such as a financial plan describing how the plan would be funded, project lists, or cost estimates.

Specifically, fewer than half of all state DOTs (20) reported that their most recent long-range statewide transportation plan included a financial plan demonstrating fiscal constraint. According to federal planning regulations, a financial plan demonstrates consistency between reasonably available and projected sources of federal, state, local, and private revenues and the costs of implementing proposed transportation system improvements. Although state DOTs are not required to provide a financial plan in the long-range statewide transportation plan, federal law requires MPOs to provide this information in their long-range, metropolitan transportation plan. Fewer state DOTs (13) reported that they include in their long-range plan a list of specific projects to be programmed, or cost estimates for those projects (12).

These survey results are consistent with the information provided by USDOT officials and stakeholders that we interviewed, who told us that many long-range statewide transportation plans are policy-based documents that provide broad, general goals for the state, but do not provide project-level information on how the state will achieve these goals. Similarly, federal planning regulations permit long-range statewide transportation plans to be comprised of policies, strategies, or both, but not necessarily specific projects, over the minimum 20-year forecast period. State DOT officials that we interviewed provided reasons for not including project-specific information in their long-range statewide transportation plan. For example, PennDOT officials reported that they do not include such information because they do not want to duplicate or override the projects included in metropolitan transportation plans where such elements are required. USDOT officials reported that the decision whether to provide project-specific information in long-range statewide transportation plans offers trade-offs to states. For example, including projects in long-range plans can provide a greater level of transparency into the state's project selection process; however the public may see these plans as the final decision-making process, giving state DOTs less flexibility to alter the plan in the future.

State DOTs Conduct Several Research and Funding Allocation Activities to Develop the STIP and Base Project Selection on a Range of Factors

In developing a STIP—the list of projects prioritized by the state to receive federal funding over a 4-year period—state DOTs reported performing several activities to assess transportation needs and determine funding allocation amounts. After completing these activities, state DOTs reported they base their selection of projects on a range of factors, including funding availability and priorities established by the governor, as well as political and public support for specific projects.

STIP Development Activities

Research to assess needs. State DOTs commonly reported assessing their transportation needs by using available transportation data and by meeting with local officials in state regions—activities that they also reported performing in developing their long-range statewide transportation plans. Forty-three state DOTs reported reviewing the condition of existing transportation assets to identify those with the greatest need, and the same number of state DOTs also reported meeting with local officials in state regions to determine needs.[26] For example, MDOT officials reported that Montana uses a “Performance Programming Process” to assess areas of need based on pavement, bridge, highway-safety and congestion data collected by the state. The planners use the data to develop an optimal funding allocation program based on needs, and district engineers, in consultation with local elected officials across the state, nominate projects for inclusion in the STIP.

Allocating funding. Through our survey and interviews with state DOT officials, we found that state DOTs used a combination of approaches to determine how to allocate available funding across competing transportation needs and state regions. For example, 47 state DOTs reported allocating funding across different project types, such as bridge or road maintenance, or transit projects. Forty state DOTs reported allocating transportation funding across geographic regions based on need, and 35 reported using predetermined formulas to allocate funding to different regions in the state. Although formula allocations may help states decide how to distribute funding across competing regions, we have previously reported that the use of formulas to distribute federal highway funds to states results in federal allocations that have only an indirect relationship to needs and no relationship to performance or outcomes.[27] In some cases, state DOTs use formula allocations that consider needs to distribute STIP funding. For example, PennDOT officials said that, as a general rule, they attempt to allocate at least 80 percent of state and federal transportation funding toward preservation and maintenance activities, while applying much of that funding toward reducing the number of structurally deficient bridges in the state. Within its bridge program, PennDOT uses formulas to distribute federal and state funding to planning regions based on the percentage of bridge deck area in the region considered to be structurally deficient, with a goal of allocating 85 percent of bridge money to improve structurally deficient bridges.

STIP Project Selection Factors

State DOTs reported that they select projects for inclusion in their STIP based on a range of factors, but funding availability and political and public support were of greater importance than the results of economic analysis of a transportation project's benefits. Economic analysis was one of the factors that state DOTs cited less often as important in selecting STIP projects (see figure 4). In addition, state DOTs must incorporate the approved TIPs of MPOs within the state, without change, into the STIP.

Funding availability. Nearly all state DOTs reported that the availability of federal and state funds was of great or very great importance in determining which projects to include in the STIP, as the amount of funding that is available determines the number and scale of projects that the state can undertake. As noted in our prior work, although transportation revenues have, until recently, increased in nominal terms, the federal and state motor fuel tax rates have not kept up with inflation; and the purchasing power in real terms of revenues generated by federal and state motor fuel taxes has been declining since 1990.[28] Consequently, state and regional transportation decision makers in recent years have devoted more funding to highway investments that preserve, enhance, and maintain existing infrastructure than to investments that add capacity. Most state DOTs (46) also cited the availability of state or local funds to match federal funds as being of great or very great importance in selecting STIP projects. For example, West Virginia DOT (WVDOT) officials told us that WVDOT is responsible for maintaining 92 percent of the road miles in the state, and because many of the counties in the state are economically distressed they are unable to provide a local match for local road improvements.

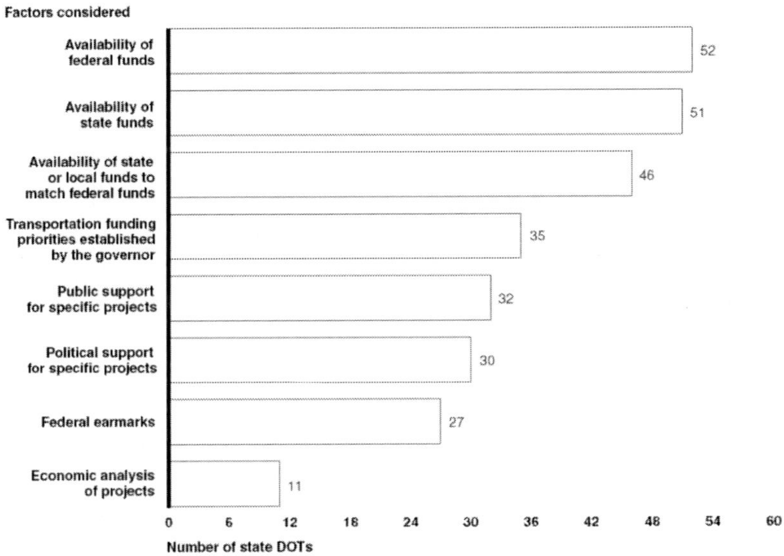

Source: State DOT survey.

Note: Data collected for additional categories were not included in this figure. See the e-supplement—GAO-11-78SP—for additional information.

Figure 4. Selected Factors State DOTs Reported Were of Great or Very Great Importance in Decisions to Include Projects in the STIP.

Governor's priorities and political and public support. About two-thirds (35) of state DOTs also identified the governor's funding priorities as a factor of great or very great importance in selecting transportation projects. For example, Pennsylvania's governor set a goal to reconstruct or replace 1,145 bridges in the state by 2010, and PennDOT's most recent STIP indicates that in fiscal year 2009, PennDOT allocated almost half of its STIP funding toward bridge projects. Other STIP project selection factors that more than half of state DOTs cited as being of great or very great importance were public (32) and political (30) support for specific transportation projects. For example, in interviews with officials at Washington state DOT, we learned that the state legislature increased state gas tax revenues by 5 cents per gallon in 2003 and by 9.5 cents per gallon over a 4-year period in 2005, raising about $11 billion for highway, bridge, ferry, and other improvements. To help raise support for the tax increases, state legislators needed to identify for voters the specific projects to be funded with the tax revenues, and the legislature, with assistance from the Washington state DOT, wrote the projects into the state legislation.

Federal earmarks. The majority of state DOTs (27) also reported that federal earmarks, also known as congressional directives, were of great or very great importance in selecting STIP projects.[29] In 2007, the USDOT Inspector General reported that SAFETEA-LU included a total of 7,808 earmarks for fiscal year 2006 for FHWA and FTA programs, accounting for just more than $8 billion.[30] FHWA and FTA provide such funds through grants to state and local agencies, which then must include the earmarked projects in the STIP to be implemented.[31] In prior work on the administration of federal earmarks within USDOT and other federal agencies, FHWA and FTA officials reported that earmarks can sometimes displace higher priority projects with lower priority projects in order to comply with these earmarks.[32] In our review, FHWA officials in one division office told us that some projects funded through federal earmarks may circumvent the statewide planning process by funding projects that are not state priorities. In addition, federal earmarks may provide only partial or initial funding for a project, leaving the state and local governments to obtain future funding to complete a project and cover future maintenance costs.

Economic analysis. In our survey, we found that economic analysis was one of the factors that state DOTs cited less often as important in selecting STIP projects (see figure 4). Eleven state DOTs reported that the results of economic analyses of STIP projects—such as benefit-cost, cost-effectiveness, or economic-impact analysis—were of great or very great importance in selecting projects.[33] According to FHWA guidance, economic analysis takes a long-term view of infrastructure performance and costs and enables state DOTs to target scarce resources to the best uses (those that maximize benefits to the public) and to account for their decisions.[34] In the planning process, economic analysis can be applied with collected performance data to make project selection more performance based by screening project alternatives based on expected performance benefits—such as reductions in travel time—with expected costs for implementing an alternative. In prior work, we found that state DOT decisions about transportation investments are based on many things besides the results of economic analysis of a project's benefits and costs, such as the availability of funding or public perception of a project.[35] Although federal planning regulations do not specify analytical tools to be applied for evaluating project merits—nor do they require that the most cost-beneficial projects be chosen—such analyses, when combined with other selection factors, including needs expressed by the community and local officials, can result in better-informed transportation investment decision-making.

USDOT has taken steps in recent years to encourage states to conduct economic analyses, including benefit-cost analysis, to plan for new transportation investments. For example, the American Recovery and Reinvestment Act of 2009 appropriated approximately $1.5 billion for competitively awarded surface transportation projects intended to have a significant impact on the nation, a metropolitan area, or a region.[36] USDOT distributed this funding through its Transportation Investment Generating Economic Recovery (TIGER) grant program. In administering the TIGER program, USDOT generally required state and other grant applicants to conduct benefit-cost analyses that compared a project's expected benefits to its costs, by measuring factors such as the project's impact on fuel savings, travel time, greenhouse gas emissions, water quality, and public health. Although we have not reviewed the economic analyses performed by states as part of this work, according to USDOT, grant requests were not approved if USDOT concluded that project costs would likely exceed public benefits.

States Use Several Methods to Consult with Nonmetropolitan Local Officials, and the Majority of Surveyed RPOs Are Satisfied That State DOTs Sufficiently Consider Their Needs

State DOTs reported using several methods to consult with nonmetropolitan local officials during the statewide planning process. Many state DOTs reported consulting directly with local elected officials, while others reported relying on RPOs to consult with nonmetropolitan local officials. In some cases, states reported that they both consult directly with local elected officials and use RPOs.

Direct consultation. The majority of state DOTs reported that they consult directly with nonmetropolitan local officials. For example, 39 state DOTs reported that they hold annual planning meetings with nonmetropolitan local officials in their state. For example, state DOT and local planning officials told us that these meetings may occur either in a series of formal state DOT presentations at various locations throughout the state (often referred to as road shows) or less formally through regular interactions between state DOT district engineers and local elected officials on an as-needed basis. According to local officials in three of the states we visited, the quality of this direct consultation can vary. For example, an official for an organization representing councils of government in one state said that each state DOT transportation district has a separate consultation process, which is effective in some districts but not in others. In another state, local officials said that their state DOT's road show, which the state uses as a way to consult with local officials, was not an effective form of consultation because many of the decisions on transportation projects had already been made by state DOT headquarters officials.

Consultation through RPOs. Fewer states reported using RPOs to fulfill consultation requirements or to perform specific planning consultation activities at the local level. In some cases, states have formalized their relationships with these organizations through written contractual agreements, while in other cases, they have no formal agreements in place. Almost half of all state DOTs (25) reported having written contractual agreements with RPOs to consult with local officials in nonmetropolitan areas (see figure 5). Fifteen state DOTs reported that they gave their RPOs a role in the planning process by requiring the RPOs to develop their own long-range plans or TIPs. In addition to the 25 state DOTs that reported having written contractual agreements with RPOs, 11 state DOTs reported that other organizations conduct rural transportation planning activities in their state without a contract. (For more information on RPO characteristics and activities, see app. II.)

Stakeholders and officials we interviewed offered some potential reasons for the greater prevalence of RPOs in some states and described some of the benefits of RPOs. For example, one stakeholder said that RPOs are more prevalent in nonmetropolitan regions with growing populations that require a coordinated planning effort to manage growth. A state DOT official in one state with a slowly growing population added that the state DOT does not see much need for formal consultation organizations because the state's slow population growth creates relatively little demand for consultation on new transportation projects. Stakeholders that we interviewed reported that RPOs help state DOTs carry out their responsibility for consulting with local nonmetropolitan officials by, for example, (1) helping competing jurisdictions develop consensus on and prioritize regional transportation projects to be included in the STIP, (2) facilitating state DOT consultation with elected officials from multiple local governments, and (3) helping state DOTs better anticipate project challenges such as issues with environmental reviews for implementing projects.

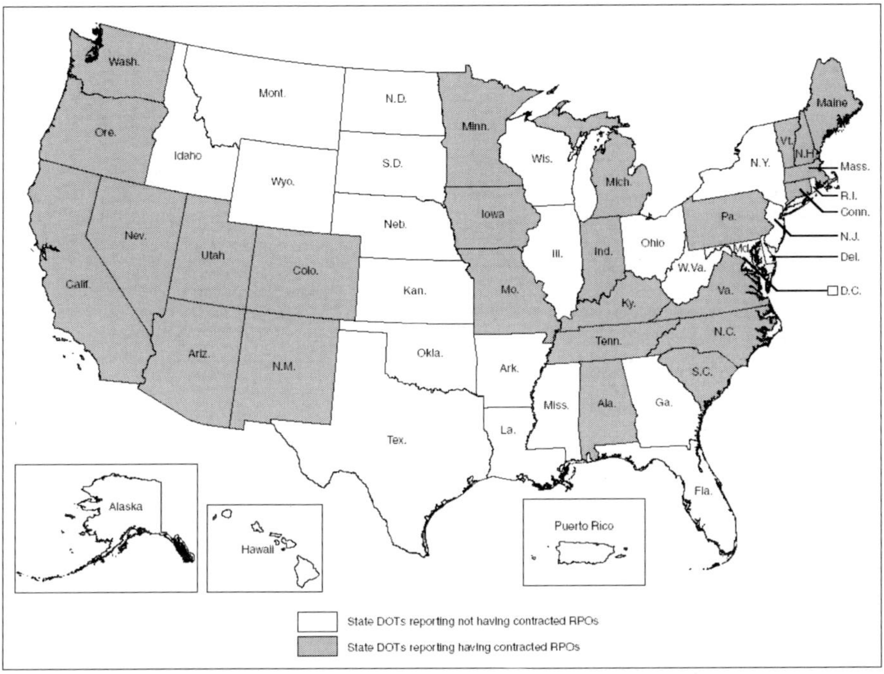

Sources: State DOT survey and Map Resources (map).

Figure 5. State DOTs That Reported Having Written Contractual Agreements with RPOs.

RPO Views on the Extent to Which Rural Transportation Needs Are Considered

In our separate survey of RPOs, 63 percent reported that they were either satisfied or very satisfied that the state DOT's consultation process gave their transportation needs sufficient consideration. In general, RPOs reported more satisfaction than their counterparts if they had helped prioritize rural projects for their area or had received planning funds or a written contractual agreement from their state DOT.

Through our survey, we also asked RPOs about their participation in certain state DOT planning activities. The majority of respondents with relevant experience reported being satisfied or very satisfied with their ability to participate in several state DOT research and outreach planning activities; however, the RPOs that responded expressed lower levels of satisfaction with their participation in other activities, including those that involve prioritizing or allocating funds for rural areas (see figure 6).

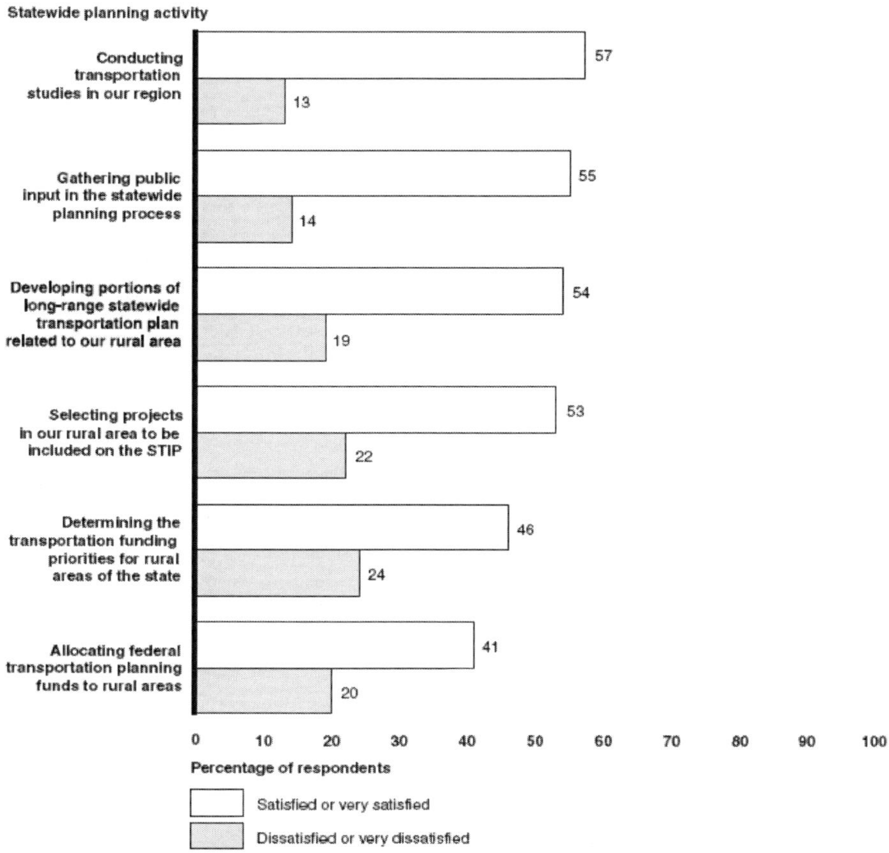

Source: Regional planning and development organization survey.

Note: Data collected for additional categories were not included in this figure. See the e-supplement—GAO-11-78SP—for the complete list of frequencies for each survey question. Some survey respondents indicated that they were neither satisfied nor dissatisfied with their participation in these activities, and that information is not included in this figure.

Figure 6. Percentages of RPOs That Reported Satisfaction and Dissatisfaction with Their Ability to Participate in Selected Statewide Planning Activities.

RPO officials we interviewed in some states expressed varying degrees of satisfaction with their ability to participate in statewide planning activities. For example, RPO officials in one state that reported having written contractual agreements with its RPOs, reported that the state DOT was generally receptive to the projects that the RPO included in their TIP and made efforts to ensure that RPO projects were considered for funding. RPO officials in this state said that the state DOT and the RPOs work together early in the planning process to agree on the statewide funding priorities. RPOs then use this information to develop projects that address the statewide priorities. However, in another state, where the RPOs also had written contractual agreements with the state DOT, an RPO official said that, although RPOs are required to develop both long- and short-range transportation plans for their regions, the state DOT does not necessarily use their project recommendations to select STIP projects. Other RPO officials said that they did not know how the state DOT ultimately selected its STIP projects and that they were unable to influence decision-making to ensure their RPO's needs were considered.

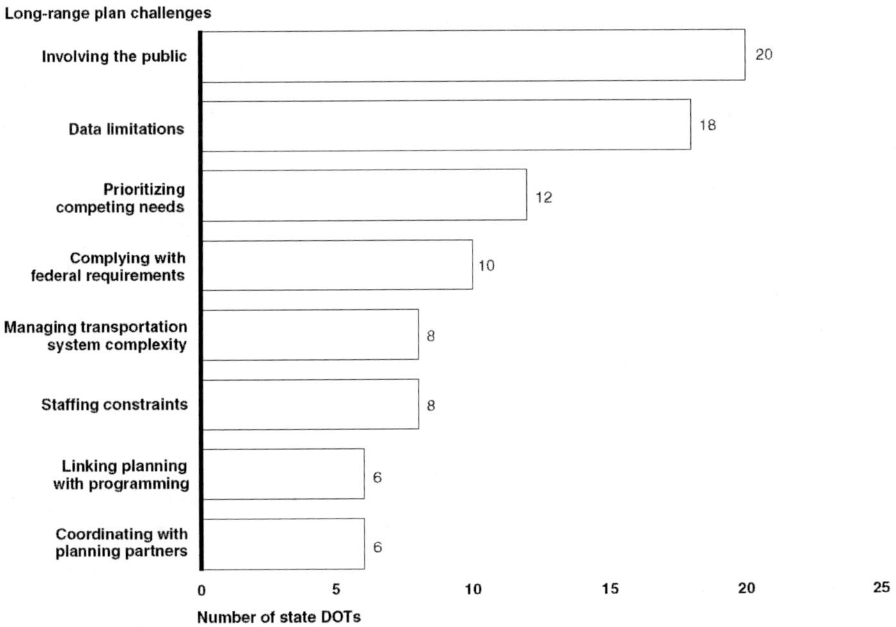

Source: State DOT survey.

Note: In addition to the challenges provided in this figure, state DOTs commonly identified funding challenges in developing the long-range statewide transportation plan, as noted previously in this report. Specifically, 17 state DOTs identified both insufficient funding and funding and cost uncertainty as significant challenges faced in developing the long-range statewide transportation plan.

Figure 7. Number of State DOTs That Identified the Following among Their Most Significant Challenges Encountered in Developing the Long-Range Statewide Transportation Plan.

Funding, Public Involvement, and Administrative Requirements Are the Primary Challenges in Statewide Planning

State DOTs Report Facing Funding Challenges in Developing Long-Range Plans and STIPs

In our survey, we asked each of the 52 state DOTs, including Washington, D.C. and Puerto Rico, to identify the top three challenges that they encountered in developing both their long-range statewide transportation plans and their STIPs.[37] When we combined the state DOTs' responses for both plans, two funding challenges emerged as the state DOTs' top challenges: (1) insufficient funds from federal or state and local sources to meet their transportation project needs and (2) funding and cost uncertainty—including uncertainty forecasting future revenues and costs for implementing transportation projects. However, these funding challenges are the result, at least in part, of revenue decisions made at the state and local levels. For example, one strategy that Congress has used to meet the goals of the Federal-Aid Highway Program has been to increase federal investment.[38] However, as we have previously reported, states and localities are permitted to use increased federal funds to substitute for or replace what they otherwise would have spent from state resources. As a result, not all of the increased federal investment has increased the total investment in highways.[39]

Transportation needs outweigh available funds. Seventeen state DOTs cited insufficient funds to meet state-defined transportation project needs as being among their most significant challenges in developing the long-range statewide transportation plan and 22 state DOTs cited insufficient funds to meet project needs as being among their most significant STIP development challenges.[40] In both cases, the state DOTs were referring to funding available to implement projects, not to conduct statewide planning activities. DOT officials from several states said that their transportation needs outweighed their existing revenue, in part because of reduced or stagnant revenues from state gas taxes coupled with demand for maintaining aging transportation infrastructure. Several state DOTs reported that insufficient funding requires planners to make difficult trade-offs between preserving existing assets and modernizing transportation networks to address future concerns such as increased congestion or livability and mobility. FTA officials reported that because of insufficient funds for transit, there are few large transit expansion projects in development across the country.[41] Consequently, most planning for transit occurs within the transit agencies as they look for ways to reconfigure their existing routes to adapt to population patterns and maximize service levels for existing routes.

Funding and cost uncertainty. Seventeen state DOTs cited funding and cost uncertainty as a significant long-range planning challenge, and 15 state DOTs cited it as a significant STIP development challenge. In survey responses and interviews, officials from several state DOTs reported that uncertain funding levels from both federal and state sources hindered their ability to address long- and short-range planning needs. For example, officials from one state DOT reported that funding uncertainty is a particular challenge as many transportation projects span multiple years and thus require careful long-range planning to prevent exhaustion of funding prior to their completion. Officials from several state DOT's reported that a lack of a federal surface transportation authorization also contributed to funding uncertainty. Furthermore, USDOT officials reported that some state legislatures place restrictions on how state gas tax funds may be spent, which limits states' flexibility in allocating their limited budgets from year to year. Several other state DOTs reported that they experienced challenges developing accurate cost estimates for projects, especially when developing the STIP. For example, officials in one state reported that, until recent years, planners did not have access to useful cost estimating tools to project future project costs. Without such cost-estimating tools, officials reported that project selection and funding decisions were made outside the planning process and subject to political interests. Officials reported that the state has recently made investments to upgrade its cost-estimating capabilities to prioritize the most cost-effective and greatest need pavement and bridge projects; thereby improving the role of planning to inform project selection decisions.

State DOTs Face Challenges Involving the Public, Addressing Data Limitations, and Other Long-Range Issues

In addition to funding challenges, state DOTs identified several significant long-range planning challenges. Twenty state DOT's reported that involving the public in the long-range planning process was a significant challenge. In addition, 18 state DOTs cited data limitations—including insufficient data and challenges analyzing and modeling data—as a significant long-range planning challenge. Fewer state DOTs identified prioritizing competing needs, complying with federal requirements, and other issues as significant long-range planning challenges (see figure 7).

Involving the public. Through our survey and interviews, state DOTs identified several challenges encountered in involving the public in long-range planning, as well as several activities commonly used by states to improve public involvement. First, several state DOTs reported that they experienced challenges in getting the public to attend long-range planning outreach sessions, in part because of the long-range plan's 20-year horizon and, in some cases, a lack of project-specific information. For example, in developing its current long-range statewide transportation plan, one state DOT reported that it held about 20 public meetings and workshops across the state; however, less than a dozen members of the public attended meetings in some rural areas of the state. Another state DOT reported that the methods it used to solicit public feedback—public notices or display ads in newspapers—were ineffective because of reduced newspaper readership and constraints on spending to purchase such ads.

State DOTs reported conducting a variety of activities to address the challenge of involving the public. In particular, 46 state DOTs reported maintaining a Web site to provide public information and receive public feedback on the long-range statewide transportation plan, and slightly fewer (42) reported presenting their long-range statewide transportation plan in a statewide road show. States also reported that they took steps to involve hard-to-reach populations and special interests. For example, 39 state DOTs reported that they reached out to special needs populations—including low-income, disabled, and elderly residents—and 37 state DOTs reported holding meetings with freight industry representatives on their long-range plan. To identify transportation needs for nonmetropolitan areas of the state when developing the long-range plan, 37 state DOTs reported that they tasked DOT personnel or contractors to perform this activity, and fewer (24) relied on RPOs to identify such needs.

Data limitations. State DOTs identified several types of data limitations as a significant challenge in developing the long-range statewide transportation plan. Specifically, 13 state DOTs identified analyzing and modeling existing data as a significant challenge, and 5 state DOTs identified insufficient data as such a challenge. For example, 3 state DOTs reported challenges gathering or making use of truck freight data in developing the long-range statewide transportation plan, such as in segregating freight trips from passenger traffic in analyzing corridor studies. Other long-range planning data challenges identified by state DOTs include the costliness of collecting data, retaining adequate staff, a lack of analytical tools to model and analyze data, and developing and using performance measures in the long-range statewide transportation plan.

Other long-range planning challenges. Among the other long-range planning challenges identified, 12 state DOTs reported that prioritizing competing needs—such as the needs of urban and rural areas—was a significant challenge. For example, in interviews with state DOT officials and other stakeholders, we learned that rural areas are likely to advocate for corridor projects or improvements to support economic development in their region, while urban areas often focus on reducing congestion or adding capacity. Eight state DOTs reported facing staffing challenges, including 2 state DOTs that reported they have insufficient staff to address the long-range statewide transportation plan among their other planning activities.

State DOTs Face Compliance, Administrative, and Other Challenges in Developing the STIP

In addition to funding challenges, almost half of state DOTs (22) cited complying with federal requirements, including demonstrating fiscal constraint and others, as a significant STIP development challenge. Fewer state DOTs (16) identified administrative challenges with maintaining the STIP, including updating the STIP to reflect amendments or other modifications, as a significant challenge. Other frequently mentioned STIP challenges were prioritizing competing needs—a commonly cited long-range planning challenge—and coordinating with planning partners, such as MPOs or RPOs (see figure 8).

Complying with federal requirements. A total of 22 state DOTs cited challenges related to complying with federal requirements in developing the STIP. In particular, 13 state DOTs cited challenges demonstrating fiscal constraint—a federal requirement that states demonstrate that all projects on the STIP can be implemented using committed, available, or reasonably available revenue sources. Two stakeholders that we interviewed reported that some FHWA division offices interpret the fiscal constraint rule rigidly and require states to provide very detailed cost and revenue estimates, while others allow for greater flexibility in their review to account for limitations in developing accurate estimates of future revenues and project costs. Despite the challenge that demonstrating fiscal constraint presents to state DOTs, FHWA officials reported that it serves an important accountability and transparency function in that it requires states to set reasonable expectations among MPOs and the public about which projects can be implemented given available revenues. In addition to challenges with demonstrating fiscal constraint, 9 state DOTs cited complying with other planning requirements—such as ensuring that a state's MPOs complete required air-quality conformity analyses—as a significant challenge.

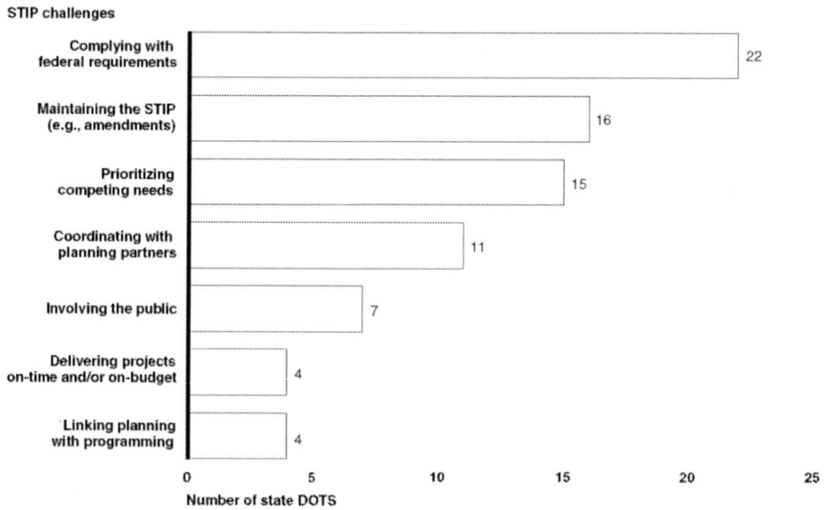

Source: State DOT survey.

Note: Complying with federal requirements includes demonstrating fiscal constraint (identified by 13 state DOTs) and other federal requirements (identified by 9 state DOTs). In addition to the challenges provided in this figure, state DOTs also commonly identified several funding challenges in developing the STIP, as noted previously in this report. Specifically, 22 state DOTs identified funding insufficiency, 15 state DOTs identified funding and cost uncertainty, and 5 state DOTs identified funding inflexibility as significant challenges faced in developing the STIP.

Figure 8. Number of State DOTs That Identified the Following among Their Most Significant Challenges Encountered in Developing the STIP.

Maintaining the STIP. About a third of state DOTs (16) reported that maintaining the STIP (e.g., amending the STIP as changes occur) was a significant administrative challenge. Federal planning regulations allow states to add or delete projects on the STIP or to revise project cost estimates at any time. In general, major changes to STIP project costs, initiation dates, or scope are known as amendments, and minor changes are considered administrative modifications.[42] STIP amendments require the state DOT to provide a public comment period and demonstrate that the STIP remains fiscally constrained for FHWA and FTA approval.[43] According to data collected by FHWA division offices, in fiscal year 2009 some states made a substantial number of amendments to their STIPs for that year. For example, FHWA's New York Division reported that it approved more than 2,000 amendments to the New York DOT's STIP in fiscal year 2009, and FHWA's Pennsylvania Division office approved 500 amendments to PennDOT's STIP for that same year. According to FHWA officials we interviewed, states often have good reasons for making such amendments—particularly in fiscal years 2009 and 2010, when states needed to plan projects for significant amounts of federal funding made available by the American Recovery and Reinvestment Act of 2009. Furthermore, some states, such as New York and Pennsylvania, have more assets and older infrastructure than other states, which could necessitate more frequent maintenance and repairs and STIP amendments, according to FHWA officials.

Other STIP challenges. Almost a third of state DOTs (15) reported that prioritizing competing needs was a significant STIP development challenge—a challenge also identified by 12 states in developing their long-range statewide transportation plans, as previously reported. Fewer states cited coordinating with planning partners (11) as a significant challenge. For example, in our survey 1 state DOT reported that it has 27 planning partners, including MPOs and RPOs that develop their own TIPs and are responsible for programming some federal-aid highway funds in their own regions. The state reported that it is challenging to coordinate the development of 27 TIPs and consolidate those projects into one STIP. Other less frequently cited STIP development challenges by state DOTs include involving the public (7), delivering transportation projects on time and on budget (4), and linking planning and programming (4).

USDOT HAS LIMITED OVERSIGHT AUTHORITY OF LONG-RANGE STATEWIDE TRANSPORTATION PLANS, AND STIP OVERSIGHT FOCUSES ON PROCESS

USDOT Has Limited Oversight Authority of Long-Range Statewide Transportation Plans, and Some States' Plans Are Updated Infrequently

USDOT has limited oversight authority over long-range statewide transportation plans. Federal planning regulations require states to continually evaluate, revise, and periodically update the long-range statewide transportation plan; however, regulations do not prescribe a schedule or time frame for those updates. In addition, although USDOT is not required to review or approve long-range statewide transportation plans, states must provide copies of any new or amended long-range statewide transportation plans to USDOT for informational purposes.[44] This requirement differs from the requirement for MPOs in developing the long-range metropolitan transportation plan, which must be updated on a predetermined schedule every 4 or 5 years.[45]

Through our survey, we found that state DOTs vary in how often they update their long-range statewide transportation plan, and some states reported infrequent updates. Twenty-one state DOTs reported issuing an updated long-range statewide transportation plan within 5 years of their previously issued plan. However, 18 state DOTs reported taking between 6 and 10 years to update their plan, and 7 state DOTs reported taking 11 years or more to do so (see figure 9).[46] Five other state DOTs reported that they had issued one plan and had thus never updated that plan. Of those state DOTs that reported updating their plan at least once, the average amount of time between updates was about 7 years. However, the amount of time reported between updates varied considerably, from 2 years to as many as 18 years.

State DOT and USDOT officials offered several reasons for infrequently updating the long-range statewide transportation plan: (1) two state DOTs reported they have insufficient staff to address the long-range statewide transportation plan among their other planning priorities; (2) one state DOT reported that it had updated its plan, but the plan was not adopted by the state's transportation commission and legislature; and (3) USDOT officials said some states issue what they referred to as policy-based plans that are not updated regularly because they do not include projects and therefore do not change much over time. USDOT officials suggested that if state DOTs were required to include project-specific information in their plans, plans would likely be updated more regularly.

State DOT and FHWA officials reported that periodic updates to the long-range statewide transportation plan offer important benefits to state DOTs and the public, including setting realistic public expectations for what the state DOT can expect to accomplish. For example, officials with one state DOT that we interviewed told us that it recently completed an update of the state's plan issued in 2002. The update was prompted by a new governor and a review of the existing plan, which found that the plan included approximately $20 to $30 billion worth of projects that had not been funded or implemented because of insufficient revenues. In updating the plan, the state DOT focused its public outreach and consultations with local officials on setting more realistic expectations for future investments. The recently issued, updated plan includes a funding scenario based on current, flat revenue expectations, and identifies four key corridors in the state where improvements could be made, subject to additional revenues. Similarly, FHWA officials that we interviewed told us that, although a state's long-range plan is vital for setting and communicating the state's future transportation goals and strategies, the process of updating the long-range plan is equally important to the state DOT as the final document itself. Officials noted that states that take a committed approach to planning—such as by continually monitoring system performance, conducting ongoing research, and reaching out to the public and stakeholders—increase the likelihood of developing a plan that stakeholders will accept.

While regularly updating the long-range statewide transportation plan has inherent benefits, infrequently updating it presents several risks:

- *Infrequent updates limit USDOT's ability to determine whether states are using federal planning funds effectively to address long-range planning needs.* State DOTs receive substantial amounts of funding from FHWA and FTA for statewide planning, including funds for developing long-range statewide transportation plans. For example, in fiscal year 2009, FHWA provided $682 million in SPR funds to state DOTs to support their planning activities, including developing long-range statewide transportation plans and STIPS and annually collecting and reporting pavement condition and other data to FHWA's HPMS program. States must document and annually report on activities that they propose to be accomplished with SPR funds, and FHWA must approve these activities.[47] In our survey, four states reported not completing an update of their long-range statewide transportation plan between 2000 and 2009. In that 10-year period, those states received approximately $640 million in state planning funds, an average of $16 million per state over that period.[48] Because those states did not update their long-range statewide transportation plan over that period, it is unclear how they applied SPR funding to address their long-range planning needs. It is also unclear whether the investment decisions made over that period were based on the states' current transportation goals and strategies.

- *Some plans may not reflect the current federal surface transportation authorization.* Federal surface transportation authorization legislation creates new planning requirements and funding opportunities that states should address in their long-range statewide transportation plans. For example, through SAFETEA-LU, which was enacted in August 2005, Congress revised several federal planning provisions and established several new funding programs for state DOTs to consider in their planning process.[49] Among these were three federal transportation programs designed to target funds to infrastructure projects that have high costs, involve national or regional impacts, and cannot easily or specifically be addressed within existing federal surface transportation programs.[50] In responding to our survey, 10 state DOTs reported that they have not updated their long-range statewide transportation plans since 2004, prior to SAFETEA-LU's passage.[51] Consequently, those states' long-range statewide transportation plans likely do not reflect amended statewide planning requirements or consider some of the new transportation programs and funding opportunities established by SAFETEA-LU.
- *Some states' STIPs may not be consistent with state priorities in outdated plans.* According to federal planning requirements, each project included in the STIP must be consistent with the long-range statewide transportation plan. States with a long-range plan that is not periodically updated may lack a plan that has been through the public participation and consultation processes and addresses the state's current transportation conditions or provides new strategies to address changing conditions.

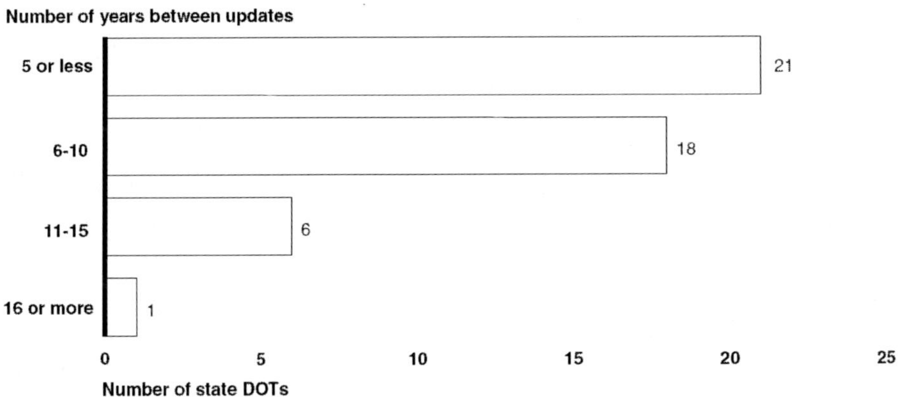

Source: State DOT survey.

Note: This figure is based on the 46 state DOTs that reported having updated their long-range statewide transportation plan at least one time. Five state DOTs reported that they had only issued one long-range statewide transportation plan and had never updated that plan. One state DOT did not provide information as to whether they had ever updated their current long-range statewide transportation plan. See the e-supplement—GAO-11-78SP—for additional information.

Figure 9. Number of Years between Updates of the Long-Range Statewide Transportation Plan as Reported by State DOTs.

USDOT's Oversight of STIPs Focuses on Process

USDOT's review and approval of state DOT STIPs is the primary means through which FHWA and FTA oversee the statewide planning process. As part of the STIP review process, state DOTs must submit to FHWA and FTA for joint review, at least every 4 years, an updated STIP, and in doing so, the state DOT must certify that its planning process was carried out in accordance with federal statutes and planning regulations, including the requirement for demonstrating fiscal constraint (see figure 1). Although there is no single, established process for conducting these joint reviews, FHWA division office personnel generally lead the STIP review process with assistance from the FTA regional office, on behalf of both agencies. They do so, in part, because FHWA division offices focus on the activities of a single state DOT, whereas FTA regional offices have multiple states in their portfolio. The majority of state DOTs submit a new STIP for FHWA's and FTA's approval either on an annual or biannual basis, and many state DOTs amend their STIP over the course of a year, requiring FHWA and FTA to review the amended document to ensure that it remains fiscally constrained. When that review is complete, FHWA and FTA send the state DOT a letter indicating that they have approved the STIP in its entirety, approved the STIP subject to certain corrective actions, or partially approved the STIP for a portion of the state.

Pursuant to federal law, USDOT's oversight of the STIP is focused on a state DOT's compliance with planning process requirements. In addition, USDOT's STIP oversight does not consider transportation planning outcomes. Specifically, through the STIP review and approval process, FHWA and FTA make a joint finding on the extent to which the STIP is based on a statewide planning process that meets or substantially meets federal planning requirements—for example, by ascertaining whether the state DOT has demonstrated fiscal constraint over the 4 years covered by the STIP. However, federal statutes or planning regulations do not require states to establish or attain specific performance thresholds or outcomes in the statewide planning process, such as improving highway safety, reducing congestion, or maintaining the state of repair of a state's transportation assets. We have previously recommended to USDOT,[52] as well as to Congress, that adopting performance measures and goals for programs can aid in measuring and evaluating the success of the programs, thereby potentially leading to better decisions about transportation investments.[53] As discussed in the next section of this report, some states do not have the performance measures and targets they would need to determine whether they have attained such thresholds or outcomes. According to USDOT officials and other stakeholders that we interviewed, FHWA and FTA's joint review of a state DOT's STIP does not evaluate the effectiveness of the state's planning process in achieving such transportation outcomes—instead, it focuses solely on whether the state has a process in place to meet federal planning requirements and whether the state-certified STIP meets those requirements. We have previously reported that, in addition to ensuring compliance with regulations, oversight provides a means by which the federal government can ensure that federal funds are being used to achieve planned outcomes. If FHWA and FTA jointly determine and document that the submitted or amended STIP does not meet federal planning requirements, FHWA and FTA can withhold future apportioned surface transportation program funds until substantial compliance is demonstrated.[54] However, USDOT's internal planning guidance indicates that, in general, FHWA and FTA do not disapprove STIPs. Instead, the planning guidance indicates that the STIP is reviewed to determine if any portion of the document meets the federal requirements and can be partially approved. In our review, we examined FHWA and FTA planning findings for the most recent STIP submitted by each of the 52 state DOTs, not including amendments. We found that FHWA and FTA approved all 52 STIPs, including 35 in their entirety, 13 subject to corrective actions, and 4 partially.[55] USDOT officials reported that in many cases, FHWA and FTA collaborate closely with the state DOT throughout the planning process and are able to address any issues that could result in a corrective action following the STIP review. As a result, FHWA and FTA officials are often familiar with the content of a STIP before they review it and the review can occur without findings.

MOST STATES REPORTED MAKING SOME USE OF PERFORMANCE MEASUREMENT FOR PLANNING, BUT A PERFORMANCE-BASED FRAMEWORK OFFERS OPPORTUNITIES TO IMPROVE STATEWIDE PLANNING

Most States Reported Using Some Performance Measures and Targets, but Several Challenges Limit Greater Use of Performance Measurement in Planning

In our survey and interviews, state DOTs reported using performance measurement—specifically performance measures and targets—in the statewide transportation planning process. Overall, the majority of state DOTs reported making use of performance data in developing their long-range statewide transportation plan (32) and their STIP (36). The most commonly used performance measures and quantifiable performance targets were reported in the areas of safety and asset condition, with lower levels of usage of project delivery and mobility measures (see table 1). Not surprisingly, state DOTs also reported that safety and asset condition measures were considered to be most useful to the statewide planning process. Although many states reported using some performance measures, stakeholders and USDOT officials told us that only a select few states have made significant attempts to integrate performance measurement into their statewide planning process to inform investment decisions.

- *Safety measures.* Almost all state DOTs (50) reported using safety measures in the past 12 months, and 49 state DOTs reported having quantifiable performance targets for these measures. Fewer state DOTs (40) considered safety measures of great or very great use in the planning process. The extensive use of safety measures is due, in part, to the federal requirement that state DOTs develop a strategic highway safety plan that establishes statewide goals and objectives to reduce highway fatalities and serious injuries on all public roads.[56] Of those state DOTs reporting that safety measures were of great or very great use, several cited crash data as being particularly useful for identifying high-crash locations or intersections and prioritizing improvements in those areas. Others reported that safety measures were used to evaluate the effectiveness of specific safety programs, such as seat belt use or motorcycle safety, or to develop the strategic highway safety plan.

- *Asset condition measures.* The vast majority of state DOTs (49) also reported using measures for the conditions of their roads, pavement, and bridges, and most of these state DOTs also reported having performance targets for these measures. The widespread availability and usage of these measures is likely related to the requirement that state DOTs collect and report data to FHWA on the condition of their roads and bridges.[57] Forty-four state DOTs considered bridge condition measures to be of great or very great use and 42 state DOTs considered road condition measures to be of great or very great use in their planning process. DOTs reported referring to these measures to make funding allocation decisions, identify assets most in need of improvement, and prioritize competing projects.
- *Project measures.* Forty-three state DOTs reported using project cost performance measures, 42 state DOTs used project timeliness performance measures, and 39 state DOTs used performance measures on progress made in implementing the STIP. Fewer state DOTs reported having performance targets for these measures, and fewer still reported that these measures were of great or very great use in statewide planning. While states are not required to use project measures, state DOTs find that monitoring project costs and timeliness can help mitigate cost overruns and project delays. For example, officials with one state DOT said that tracking how well project costs compare to project estimates enables them to schedule a high percentage of available funding based on the state DOT's history of delivering projects on time and on budget.
- *Mobility measures.* Overall, fewer state DOTs reported using performance measures or having performance targets for mobility measures, including vehicle congestion, truck freight, intermodal

connectivity, and transit congestion (see table 1). Vehicle congestion measures were the most widely used mobility measures, with 42 state DOTs reporting using these measures and 35 state DOTs reporting having quantitative performance targets for these measures. State DOTs reporting that mobility measures were of great or very great use identified several uses for the measures, including factoring congestion data into their funding allocation models and using vehicle congestion data as a preliminary screen for determining whether to widen a road in the future.

Table 1. Number of State DOTs Reporting Using Performance Measurement to Inform Decisions in the Statewide Planning Process in the Last 12 Months

	Used performance measures in the last 12 months	Had quantifiable targets for performance data	Considered to be of very great or great use to planning process
Safety and asset condition measures			
Safety measures	50	49	40
Road surface or pavement conditions	49	47	42
Bridge conditions	49	48	44
Project measures			
Project costs	43	34	29
Timeliness of project delivery	42	38	21
Progress made implementing the STIP	39	38	21
Progress made implementing long-range statewide transportation plan	33	22	12
Mobility measures			
Vehicle congestion levels	42	35	25
Truck freight mobility	32	13	12
Intermodal connectivity of state transportation network	25	12	9
Transit congestion levels	22	10	4
Other measure			
Surface transportation-related emissions or energy consumption	24	20	9

Source: State DOT survey.

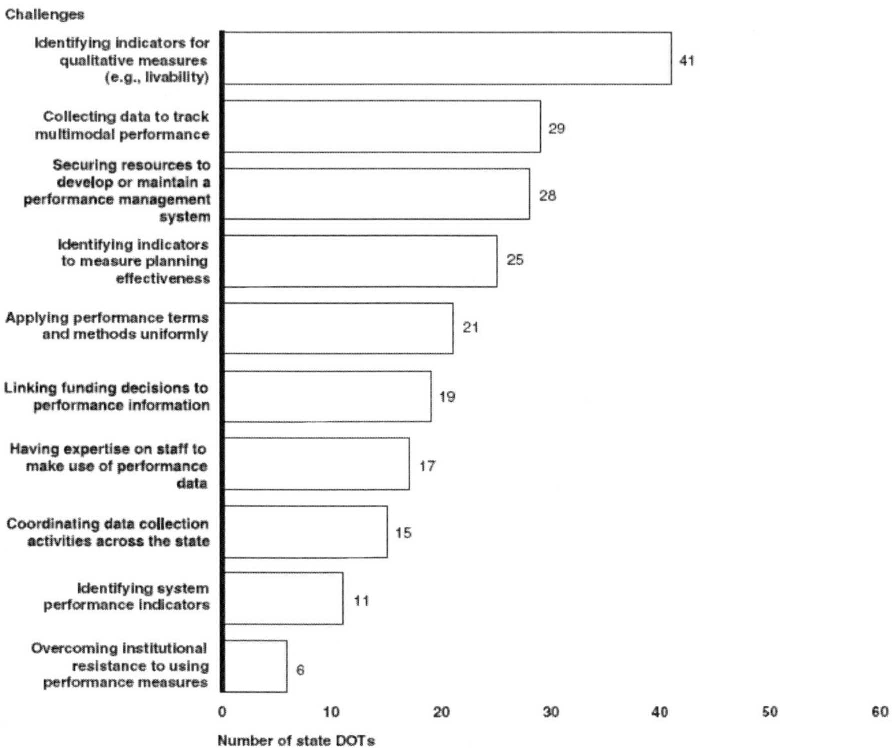

Source: State DOT survey.

Figure 10. Great or Very Great Challenges to Using Performance Measures for Transportation Planning Reported by State DOTs.

Despite efforts to use performance measures in planning, state DOTs identified several significant challenges that limit their ability to make broader use of performance measures. The challenges that state DOT's cited most frequently in our survey as being a great or very great challenge were identifying indicators for qualitative measures such as livability, collecting data to track multimodal performance, and securing sufficient resources to develop and maintain a performance management system. Only six state DOTs reported that institutional resistance to using performance measures was a great or very great challenge to using performance measures for transportation planning (see figure 10).

- *Identifying indicators for qualitative measures.* Forty-one state DOTs reported that identifying indicators for qualitative measures such as livability was a great or very great challenge. USDOT officials, stakeholders, and state DOTs that we interviewed reported that there is little consensus among states on how qualitative variables—such as livability, mobility, or congestion—should be defined or what indicators should be used to measure such concepts.[58] Congestion, for example, has several widely recognized indicators—including number of cars, delay times, and person throughput—yet no single standard exists for reliably collecting or using these data to compare performance across locales. Several stakeholders and USDOT officials noted that even for commonly collected quantitative measures, such as road and pavement surface conditions, there is a lack of consensus among state DOTs on whether pavement roughness measures or other indicators, such as remaining surface life, are most useful.

- *Collecting data to track system performance across multiple modes.* Twenty-nine state DOTs reported that collecting data to track multimodal performance—such as delay times for highway and transit travel—was a great or very great challenge. Stakeholders reported that some states do not have tools and performance measures that would allow them to consider and compare investments in strategies for managing traffic and transit operations alongside investments in more conventional highway infrastructure improvements. Moreover, although state DOTs generally collect performance data to manage state-owned transportation assets, the percentage of roads that are owned and maintained by the state DOT varies across states. Furthermore, stakeholders and state DOT officials reported that states often have insufficient data on truck or freight volumes across their transportation networks that could support long-range systemwide planning.
- *Securing sufficient resources to develop and maintain a performance management system.* In our survey, 28 state DOTs reported that securing sufficient resources for a performance management system was a great or very great challenge. As noted previously, FHWA annually apportions substantial amounts of SPR funds to states for statewide planning and research activities, including collecting data on the performance and condition of public roads for FHWA's HPMS program. In fiscal year 2009, for example, states received a total amount of more than $680 million to fund planning and research activities. Nonetheless, in our interviews, planning officials noted that collecting and maintaining such data is time-consuming and

expensive. For example, states must continually collect road and bridge condition data, which may be housed in separate databases and in different data formats. Planning officials also told us that developing the internal processes to properly collect and use data to make decisions can take many years. For example, officials at the Washington state DOT said that although they began measuring transportation asset performance in the 1990s, it took them a number of years to identify the most meaningful indicators and refine the data collection and analysis procedures to enable performance-based investment decision making. The officials reported that over time, performance management processes were implemented agency wide to address all of Washington state DOT's program and modal responsibilities.

A Performance-Based Framework Offers Opportunities to Improve Statewide Planning

Through interviews with transportation planning stakeholders and through our expert panel, we identified several elements of a performance-based framework that offer opportunities to facilitate states' use of performance measurement and improve the statewide planning process. Those elements include (1) national transportation goals, (2) collaboratively developed performance measures, (3) appropriate performance targets, and (4) revised federal oversight of statewide planning. Elements of this framework are also consistent with performance measurement requirements that apply to federal agencies, according to prior GAO work,[59] and a recent FHWA report on the experience of other countries in applying performance management to transportation programs.[60]

National transportation goals. Transportation planning stakeholders we interviewed and participants in our expert panel commonly cited clear national transportation goals as a critical ingredient in performance-based planning. According to several stakeholders, national goals are necessary to provide clear policy direction for federal transportation investments. In previous work, we have noted that for many surface transportation programs, goals are numerous and conflicting, and we recommended that Congress consider refocusing surface transportation programs so that they have well-defined goals with direct links to an identified federal interest and role.[61] FHWA's international scan report also recommends, as a first step in developing a performance measurement program, that a limited number of high-level national transportation policy goals be articulated and linked to a clear set of measures and targets, set at the state and local levels. National goals could provide states with an articulated federal interest and help states establish specific transportation outcomes in the statewide planning process, such as improving highway safety or maintaining the state of repair of a state's transportation assets. FHWA planning officials we interviewed said that national goals and associated performance measures would need to be incorporated into statewide and MPO long-range transportation plans to align state and local long-range priorities with national objectives. Such alignment would then be reflected in the STIPs and TIPs, which must be consistent with the long-range statewide transportation plans, making it easier for FHWA and FTA reviewers to ensure that federal surface transportation funds were being allocated to address national transportation goals.

Collaboratively developed performance measures. Stakeholders and panelists also commonly said that specific performance measures, linked to national goals, should be developed in close collaboration with the state and local stakeholders responsible for implementing performance-based planning. We previously reported that seeking the involvement of stakeholders and limiting the number of performance measures to a vital few are important practices in developing and implementing successful performance management systems within federal agencies.[62] Stakeholders told us that states and MPOs should be closely involved in developing appropriate performance measures because of the wide range of transportation contexts across states. Without a collaborative process to identify a vital set of performance measures that states and local planners can use, the federal government and states will lack assurance that the resources and effort directed to monitor performance will provide useful information to the federal government on the overall condition of the nation's transportation system.

While our previous work indicates that obtaining agreement among competing stakeholders in developing performance management systems is not easy, officials in one state DOT that we interviewed cited USDOT's efforts to collaborate with states on the development of appropriate performance measures. Specifically, USDOT's National Highway Traffic Safety Administration (NHTSA) partnered with the Governors Highway Safety Association (GHSA)—which represents states' highway safety offices—to jointly develop traffic safety performance measures for states to use in their strategic highway safety plans. NHTSA and GHSA brought state and local stakeholders together to develop and agree on a minimum set of 14 performance measures for states to use in developing and implementing behavioral highway safety plans and programs.[63] Participants in our expert panel suggested that FHWA and FTA could bring a national perspective and technical expertise to help states develop appropriate measures, particularly for emerging measures such as livability—a challenge that, as noted, state DOTs identified as limiting greater use of performance measurement in planning.

Appropriate performance targets. Stakeholders we interviewed and our expert panelists expressed various opinions on the value and implementation of performance targets in statewide planning. The Office of Management and Budget's guidance to federal agencies on implementing GPRA requires federal agencies to set performance goals that include performance targets and time frames, as part of the annual performance plans that federal agencies develop to show progress in achieving goals.[64] Our prior work has shown that performance targets help promote accountability and allow organizations to track their progress toward goals and give managers important information on which to base their organizational and management decisions. However, several panelists said that if performance targets were set at the federal level and if federal funding allocations were contingent on achieving those targets, states could be penalized for not achieving outcomes that could be beyond their direct control. Other panelists indicated that targets could be useful if linked to performance incentives rather than penalties, and established at the state or local level in consultation with the federal government. According to FHWA's international scan report, among the countries examined it was common for different levels of government to set performance targets jointly and collaborate on ways to achieve targets, rather than for one level of government to set a target and then penalize another for missing it.

Revised federal oversight of statewide planning. As previously noted in this report, FHWA and FTA's joint oversight of statewide planning focuses on state DOTs' compliance with planning process requirements and does not consider transportation planning outcomes. Several stakeholders and panelists told us that this process-oriented oversight is of limited value to state DOTs in improving the effectiveness of statewide planning. USDOT officials reported that a performance-based planning framework would require legislative changes to transition USDOT's statewide planning oversight role to focus on transportation outcomes, such as whether states are making progress in improving highway safety or maintaining the nation's transportation assets in a state of good repair. USDOT's recent international scan report found that linking national goals to state or regional performance measures appeared to create a strong focus on outcomes instead of process among the nations reviewed. Additionally, panelists reported that regular reporting by state DOTs to USDOT on progress made in achieving outcomes could improve communication between the states and the federal government, and enable USDOT to provide technical assistance as states' need for it becomes apparent.

Although implementing a performance-based framework will not be easy, our state DOT survey results suggest that many state DOTs could be receptive to increasing their use of performance measurement. In prior work, we have noted that the ultimate benefit of collecting performance information—improved decision making and results—is only fully realized when this information is used to support management planning and decision-making functions.[65] Our work evaluating the extent to which federal agencies' use performance information to make decisions demonstrates that such organizational change does not occur quickly.[66] However, as previously noted, only six state DOTs in our survey reported that institutional resistance to using performance measures was a great or very great challenge to using performance measures for transportation planning. Given the progress some state DOTs have already made in using performance-measurement, other state DOTs may be well-positioned to move toward a performance-based planning framework.

CONCLUSION

Statewide transportation planning is an important process for deciding how to spend substantial amounts of federal surface transportation funds—almost $46 billion in fiscal year 2009. However, the current, statewide transportation planning framework does not provide the federal government with sufficient information to ensure that states' planning activities are contributing to improved transportation outcomes—such as improving the state of repair of transportation assets—and that states are fully considering the long-range needs of the nation's transportation infrastructure. For example, because federal oversight of statewide planning focuses on process, rather than specific transportation outcomes, it is unclear whether states' investment decisions are improving the condition and performance of the nation's transportation system.

A performance-based planning framework offers opportunities to focus statewide planning on achieving transportation outcomes. Encouragingly, our state DOT survey results suggests that states have already taken some important steps in this direction by setting broad goals in their long-range statewide transportation plans and using performance measures and targets to monitor the safety and condition of many roads and bridges. However, some long-range statewide transportation plans are infrequently updated, and individual state efforts toward performance-based planning are not part of a coordinated federal approach. As a result, the federal government has limited ability to measure the results of its investment in statewide planning. Nonetheless, our results suggest that many states could be ready to transition to a performance-based planning framework, with the appropriate assistance and collaboration of the federal government. USDOT, through NHTSA, has experience working with states to make states' strategic highway safety plans more performance based. This experience could be useful to FHWA, FTA, and states as they endeavor to address both national and state transportation concerns in a performance-based planning framework. As Congress moves forward with reauthorizing federal surface transportation programs, it has an opportunity to take the legislative action needed to shift to a performance-based approach for statewide planning and oversight, through which the federal government, states, and local planners can collaboratively address their transportation concerns.

MATTERS FOR CONGRESSIONAL CONSIDERATION

Congress should consider transitioning statewide transportation planning and oversight toward a more performance-based approach. Actions to accomplish this transition could include

- identifying specific transportation outcomes for states to address in statewide transportation planning and charging USDOT with assessing states' progress in achieving these outcomes through its STIP review and approval process,
- requiring states to update their long-range statewide transportation plans on a prescribed schedule to ensure the effective use of federal planning funds and to address statewide planning outcomes, and

- requiring USDOT and states to collaboratively develop appropriate performance measures to track progress in achieving planned transportation outcomes.

AGENCY COMMENTS

We provided a draft of this report to USDOT for review and comment on November 5, 2010. USDOT officials provided technical comments which we incorporated into the report, as appropriate.

We are sending copies of this report to interested congressional committees and the Secretary of Transportation.

Sincerely yours,

Phillip R. Herr
Director, Physical Infrastructure Issues

APPENDIX I. SCOPE AND METHODOLOGY

To identify the planning activities conducted by state departments of transportation (state DOT) we reviewed federal statutes and regulations governing the statewide planning process[67] and conducted a Web-based survey of 52 state DOTs, including those in Puerto Rico and the District of Columbia. To identify survey participants, we used contacts provided by the American Association of State Highway Transportation Officials' (AASHTO) Standing Committee on Planning, current as of March 4, 2010. In designing the survey questions, we interviewed a range of transportation policy stakeholders, including state DOT planning officials and officials with the Federal Highway Administration (FHWA) and the Federal Transit Administration (FTA), and we consulted GAO staff with appropriate subject-matter expertise. In addition, we conducted three pretests of the survey of state DOTs and obtained feedback on the survey from two external planning experts and from FHWA and FTA officials to ensure that the questions were clear and did not place an undue burden on officials, that the terminology was used correctly, and that the questionnaire was comprehensive and unbiased. We made changes to the content and format of the questionnaire based on their feedback. We conducted the survey from April 20, 2010, to June 18, 2010, and received responses from all 52 state DOTs, for a 100 percent response rate. The complete results of the state DOT survey can be found at GAO-11-78SP.

Because we administered the state DOT survey to the complete universe of potential respondents, there are no sampling errors. However, the practical difficulties of conducting any survey may introduce errors, commonly referred to as nonsampling errors. For example, difficulties in how a particular question is interpreted, in the sources of information that are available to respondents, or in how the data are entered into a database or were analyzed can introduce unwanted variability into the survey results. We encountered a nonsampling survey error in analyzing the state DOT survey responses. Specifically, in some instances, respondents provided conflicting, contradictory, or unnecessary information in portions of the survey. We addressed these errors by contacting the state DOT officials involved and clarifying their responses.

To obtain more in-depth information on state DOT statewide planning activities, we reviewed planning documents from and interviewed officials in six states: Louisiana, Montana, Pennsylvania, Texas, Washington state, and West Virginia. In each state we interviewed officials from state DOTs, FHWA division offices, FTA regional offices, rural planning organizations (RPO),[68] metropolitan planning organizations (MPO), and, when present, tribal planning organizations. To ensure that we identified a range of states for our case studies, we considered

- recommendations from transportation planning stakeholders;
- the percentage of road miles owned by the state;
- the presence of MPOs in the state and the percentage of the population covered by MPOs;
- the presence of federally recognized tribes; and
- the representation of FTA regions.

These criteria allowed us, in our view, to obtain information from a diverse mix of state DOTs and other state planning organizations, but the findings from our case studies cannot be generalized to all states because the states selected were part of a nonprobability sample. We used information obtained during the case studies throughout this report.

To gather information on the extent to which RPOs are satisfied that rural needs are considered in statewide planning, we conducted a second Web-based survey of regional planning and development organizations from all 50 states.

We sent surveys to the 564 organizations in a database collected by the National Association of Development Organizations that included a range of different types of organizations that conduct regional planning activities, including RPOs, councils of government (COG), regional planning commissions, economic development agencies, county and city planning offices, and others similar organizations. Because the database did not contain organizations in Delaware, Hawaii, and Rhode Island, we identified a total of five organizations from those states that conduct regional planning activities and sent surveys to those organizations. Because the National Association of Development Organizations database includes organizations that conduct a variety of regional planning activities, including transportation planning, we asked each surveyed organization to identify the specific planning activities that it performs. In this report, we provided information only from those organizations that reported that they coordinate or conduct surface transportation or transit planning in the nonmetropolitan areas of their region. For the purposes of this report, organizations that indicated that they perform this activity are considered RPOs. To ensure the reliability of the database, we spoke with National Association of Development Organizations officials about the characteristics of the database and determined that it was sufficiently reliable for our needs. In developing the survey questions, we interviewed transportation planning stakeholders and pretested the survey with a total of five RPOs in four states to determine that the questions were clear and did not place an undue burden on officials, that the terminology was used correctly, and that the questionnaire was comprehensive and unbiased. We made changes to the content and format of the questionnaire based on their feedback. We conducted the survey from May 17, 2010, to June 25, 2010, and received completed surveys from 72 percent of the organizations surveyed. The complete results of this survey can be found at GAO-11-78SP.

To gather information on the challenges that state DOTs face in the statewide transportation planning process, we relied primarily on data collected in the state DOT survey, in which we asked state DOT respondents to identify through open-ended responses the three most significant challenges encountered in developing both the long-range statewide transportation plan and the state transportation improvement program (STIP). We then performed a content analysis on the open-ended question responses through the following process. We identified a total of 13 categories of challenges identified by state DOTs in their responses, including funding, stakeholder involvement, and staffing, among others. We developed a codebook that defined each category, and two GAO analysts independently assigned codes to each response.

Afterwards, the analysts met to resolve any differences in their coding until they reached consensus. We then removed duplicate responses—instances in which a state DOT reported the same challenge for the same plan more than once—to ensure that only unique challenges reported by state DOTs were reported in our analysis. Finally, we analyzed the coded responses to determine how many state DOTs encountered each challenge in developing both the long-range statewide transportation plan and the STIP.

To obtain information on FHWA's and FTA's approach to overseeing statewide transportation planning, we interviewed FHWA and FTA officials in headquarters and in the six states where we interviewed state DOT officials (Louisiana, Montana, Pennsylvania, Texas, Washington State, and West Virginia). Specifically, we interviewed officials in the six FHWA division offices in the six states and in the four FTA regional offices with responsibility for those states (FTA regions 3, 6, 8, and 10). We also reviewed FHWA and FTA planning guidance and the planning findings from FHWA and FTA's joint review of each state DOT's most recent STIP, to determine what joint action FHWA and FTA took following their review.

To identify the extent to which state DOTs are using performance measurement for planning and opportunities to make statewide planning more performance based, we analyzed data collected through our state DOT survey and interviews with state DOT officials. We also contracted with the National Academy of Sciences to convene a balanced, diverse panel of 14 experts to discuss performance measurement in statewide transportation planning. We worked closely with the National Academy's Transportation Research Board to identify and select panelists with experience in the implementation of performance measurement in, and knowledge of, the statewide transportation planning processes. The panelists convened in Minneapolis, Minnesota, on July 14, 2010, and their discussion was divided into three moderated subsessions. The subsessions addressed the appropriate roles of the federal government and the states in making statewide planning more performance based, how performance measures could be used to better link statewide planning to programming decisions, and the advantages and disadvantages of linking federal funding to achieving transportation performance goals. The moderator facilitated a discussion among the panelists to gather their perspectives on each topic. In keeping with the National Academy's policy, the panelists were invited to provide their individual views, and the panel was not designed to reach a consensus on any of the issues that we asked the panelists to discuss. Results of the discussions were used to inform key elements of a framework to make statewide transportation planning more performance based. We did not verify the panelists' statements. The views expressed by the panelists do not necessarily represent the views of GAO or the National Academy. Participants in the expert panel are listed in table 2.

Table 2. Panelists on the GAO and National Academy Expert Panel

Name	Affiliation
Lance Neumann (Moderator)	President, Cambridge Systematics, Inc.
Mark Aesch	Chief Executive Officer, Genesee Regional Transportation Authority (Rochester, NY)
Daniela Bremmer	Director of Strategic Assessment Washington State Department of Transportation
Leanna Depue	Director, Highway Safety Division Missouri Department of Transportation
Patricia Hendren	Director, Office of Performance Washington Metropolitan Area Transit Authority
Charles Howard	Director, Transportation Planning Puget Sound Regional Council
Tim Lomax	Research Engineer Regents Fellow Texas Transportation Institute, Texas A&M
Steve Pickrell	Senior Vice President, Policy and Planning Cambridge Systematics, Inc.
Amanda Pietz	Interim Planning and Implementation Manager Transportation Development Division, Oregon Department of Transportation
Peggy Reichert	Director, Statewide Planning and Analysis Office of Investment Management Minnesota Department of Transportation
Kyle Schneweis[a]	Chief of Governmental Affairs Kansas Department of Transportation
George Schoener	Executive Director, I-95 Corridor Coalition
Jack Stickel	Transportation Data Services Manager Alaska Department of Transportation and Public Facilities
Mary Lynn Tischer	Director, Office of Transportation Policy Studies, FHWA
David Wasserman	Transportation Engineer, Strategic Planning Office North Carolina Department of Transportation

Source: GAO.

[a]Employed by High Street Consulting on day of panel.

The expert discussion cited in this report should be interpreted in the context of two key limitations and qualifications. First, although we were able to secure the participation of a balanced, highly qualified group of experts, other experts in this field could not be included because we needed to limit the size of the panel. Although many points of view were represented, the panel was not representative of all potential views.

Second, even though GAO, in cooperation with the National Academy, conducted preliminary research and heard from national experts in their fields, a day's conversation cannot represent the current practice in this vast area. More thought, discussion, and research must be done to develop greater agreement on what we really know, what needs to be done, and how to do it. These two key limitations and qualifications provide contextual boundaries. Nevertheless, the panel provided a rich dialogue on making statewide transportation planning more performance based, and the panelists provided insightful comments in responding to the questions they were asked.

To gather additional information related to all of our research objectives, we interviewed a range of transportation planning stakeholders representing state, local, and private-sector groups, including AASHTO, the Association of Metropolitan Planning Organizations, the Bipartisan Policy Center, Cambridge Systematics Inc., the I-95 Corridor Coalition, the National Association of Counties, the National Association of Development Organizations, the National Association of Regional Councils, and National Academy's Transportation Research Board.

We conducted this performance audit from October 2009 through December 2010 in accordance with generally accepted government auditing standards. Those standards require that we plan and perform the audit to obtain sufficient, appropriate evidence to provide a reasonable basis for our findings and conclusions based on our audit objectives. We believe that the evidence obtained provides a reasonable basis for our findings and conclusions based on our audit objectives.

APPENDIX II. INFORMATION ON THE PARTICIPATION OF RURAL PLANNING ORGANIZATIONS IN STATEWIDE TRANSPORTATION PLANNING

RPOs that we surveyed reported information on the following topics discussed in this appendix:[69] (1) RPO service areas, (2) planning funds received by RPOs, (3) planning activities performed by RPOs, (4) needs of nonmetropolitan areas served by RPOs, (5) activities performed by state DOTs to consult with RPOs, and (6) RPOs' satisfaction with their state DOT's consultation activities. The complete results of this survey are available in GAO-11-78SP.

RPO Service Areas

In general, RPOs are voluntary organizations of local elected officials and representatives of local transportation systems that serve nonmetropolitan areas not represented by a metropolitan planning organization (MPO). MPOs represent urbanized areas with more than 50,000 people. However, because RPOs may serve multiple nonmetropolitan municipalities, the population of the combined RPO service areas may be greater than 50,000. In our survey, we found that the size of the population serviced by RPOs varied greatly, with 57 percent reporting a population smaller than 150,000 and 43 percent reporting a population in their service area greater than 150,000. RPOs reported, on average, that they serve 5 counties and 36 municipalities, such as cities, towns, or villages. RPOs reported that the number of full-time staff performing rural transportation planning averaged 2 and ranged from 0 to 18.

Planning Funds Received by RPOs

RPOs may receive state or federal funding to conduct nonmetropolitan planning (see table 3). Of RPOs responding to our survey, 80 percent reported receiving funding in fiscal year 2009 from their state DOT. In addition, 41 percent reported that their state DOT provided them with state planning and research (SPR) funds from FHWA and 14 percent reported that their state DOT provided them with State Planning and Research Program (SPRP) funds from FTA.

Planning Activities Performed by RPOs

We asked RPOs about the types of planning activities that they conduct. Of the 15 activities RPOs were asked about, 12 were performed by more than 50 percent of RPOs (see figure 11). More than 80 percent of RPOs reported gathering or coordinating input from public and local officials; conducting community planning activities, such as improving accessibility for seniors and disabled persons; and providing technical assistance to local governments, such as Geographic Information System mapping or transportation modeling. Most RPOs reported conducting other types of planning, such as bike and pedestrian, land-use, and transit service planning, among others. About a third to a half of RPOs reported planning for different modes, freight, or air quality and emissions and conducting other planning activities, such as tribal transportation planning, demographic forecasting, and scenic byway planning.

Needs of Nonmetropolitan Areas Served by RPOs

According to RPOs, maintaining or improving existing roads and bridges and safety are their highest-priority transportation needs. Specifically, 60 to 90 percent of RPOs reported that maintaining or improving existing roads, maintaining or improving existing bridges, and improving the safety of existing assets were of higher priority (see figure 12). Twenty-six to 29 percent reported that higher-priority needs for their region include improving public transit, such as by reducing congestion or improving accessibility; other needs, such as bike and pedestrian trails, and economic development; and improving truck freight mobility. Less than 20 percent of RPOs reported that improving rail freight mobility, increasing road or highway capacity to address congestion, or improving air quality, such as by reducing surface transportation emissions, were higher-priority needs.

Table 3. Transportation Planning Funds Received by RPOs by Source and Amount

Source[a]	Percent Reporting Receiving Funds[b]	Average Reported Amount Received	Range of Reported Amounts Received
State DOT funds	80%	$96,082	$3,000-662,000
FHWA, SPR funds	41	125,040	6,668-3,500,000
FTA, SPRP funds	14	37,919	4,000-96,745

Source: Regional Planning and Development Organization survey.

[a] FHWA SPR funds are authorized under 23 U.S.C. 505, and FTA SPRP funds are authorized under 49 U.S.C. 5305.

[b] Percent does not add up to 100 as RPOs may receive funding from more than one source.

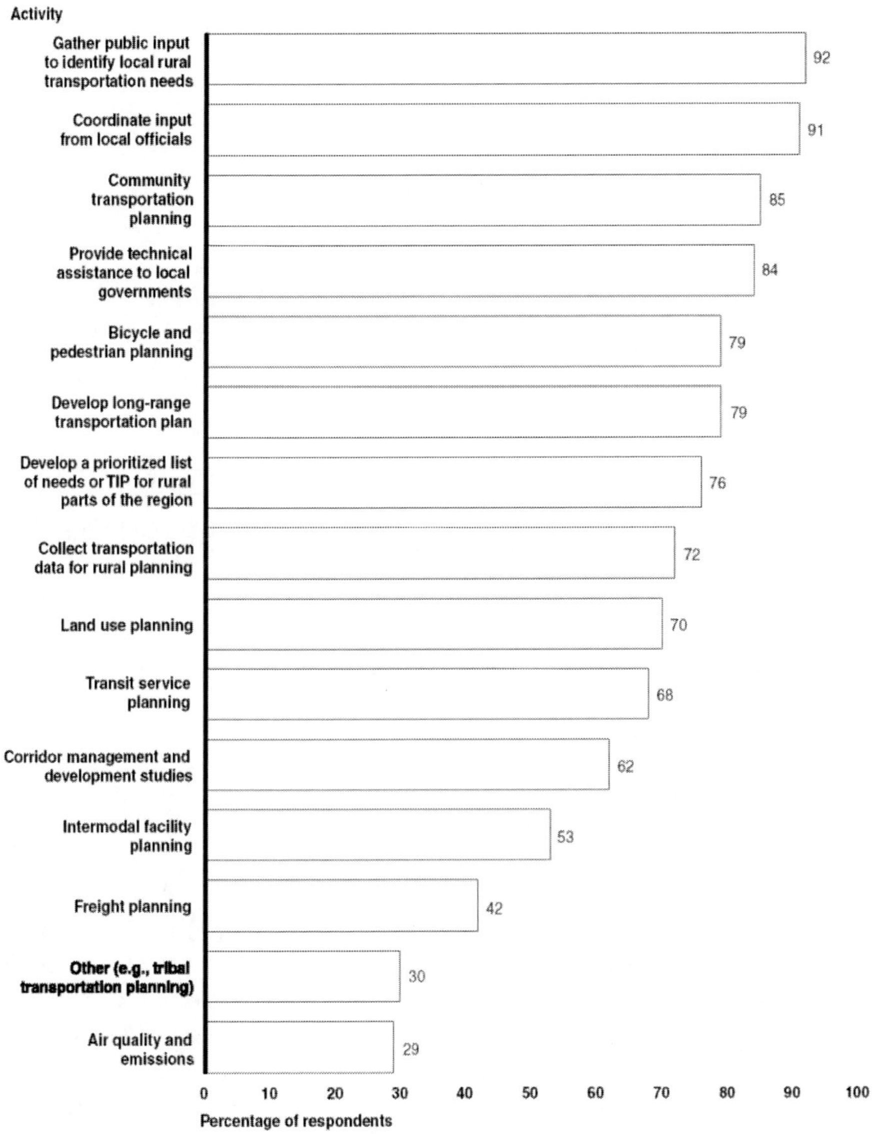

Source: Regional planning and development organization survey.

Figure 11. Survey Responses for Transportation Planning Activities Conducted by RPOs.

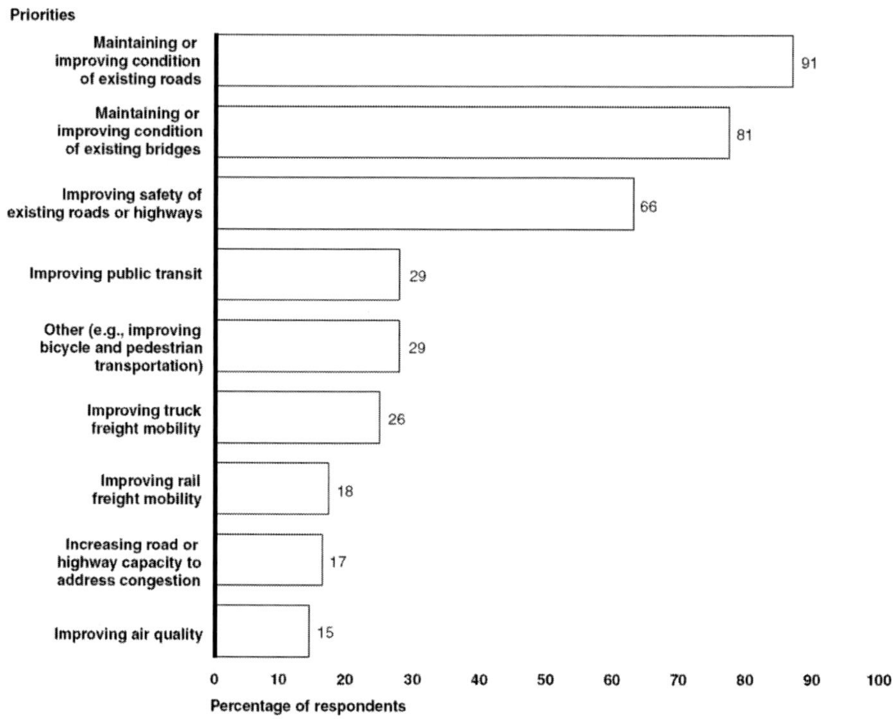

Source: Regional planning and development organization survey.

Figure 12. Survey Responses for RPOs' Opinion of the Higher-Priority Needs for the Nonmetropolitan Areas of Their Region.

Activities Performed by State DOTs to Consult with RPOs

State DOTs are required by federal guidelines to have a documented process in place to consult with nonmetropolitan areas of the state on transportation planning issues. We asked RPOs if, over the past year, their state DOT performed selected activities to consult with them in the statewide planning process. RPOs reported that their state DOT performed a wide range of different activities to consult with them. For example, 81 percent of RPOs reported that their state DOT provided funding to their region to conduct surface transportation planning activities (see figure 13). Thirty-five percent of RPOs reported that the state DOT asked local officials to serve on policy-making or advisory boards, or to participate in other activities, such as state DOT meetings to discuss specific regional projects.

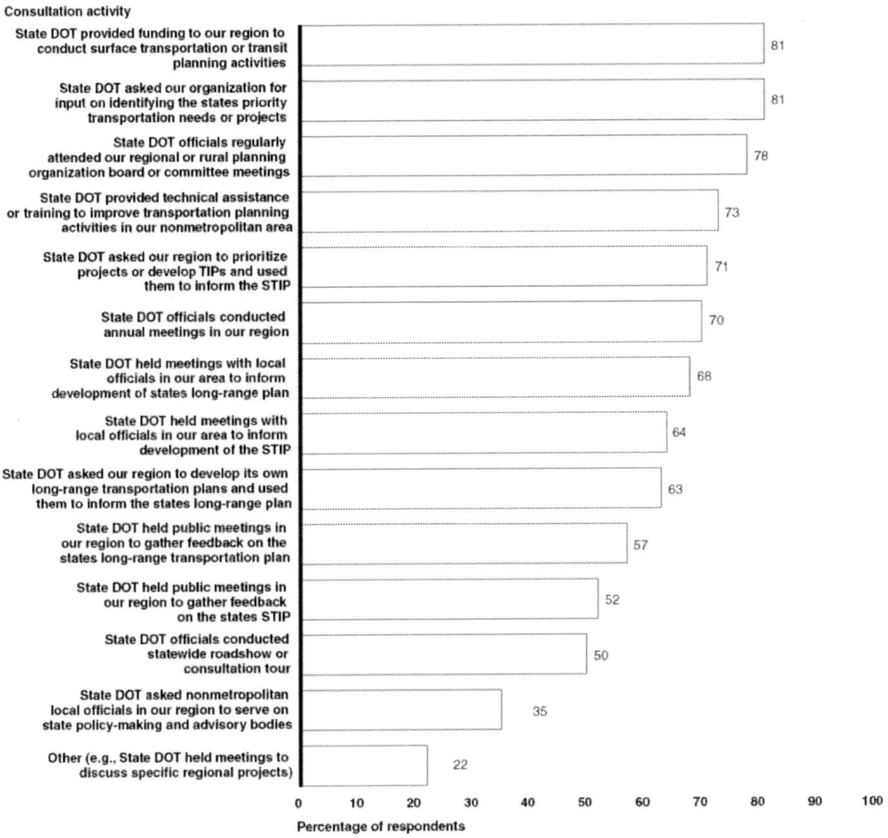

Source: Regional planning and development organization survey.

Figure 13. Survey Responses for State DOT Activities Performed to Consult with RPOs in the Statewide Planning Process.

RPOs' Satisfaction with Their State DOT's Consultation Activities

Overall, 63 percent of RPOs reported being satisfied or very satisfied that their state DOT sufficiently considers their region's needs (see page 25 of this report). However, fewer RPOs reported being satisfied or very satisfied with their ability to participate in specific state DOT consultation activities (see figure 14). More than 50 percent of RPOs reported being satisfied or very satisfied with their ability to participate in state DOT activities that gather public input in the statewide planning process, conduct transportation studies, develop portions of statewide long-range transportation plans, or select rural projects in their area to be included in the STIP. Between 30 to 46 percent of RPOs reported being satisfied or very satisfied with state DOT activities that determine the transportation funding priorities for rural areas; allocate federal planning funds to rural areas; set performance goals, measures, or targets for their area; and develop transportation models to inform decisions.

Overall, 16 percent of RPOs reported being dissatisfied or very dissatisfied with their state DOT sufficiently considers their region's needs. Dissatisfaction with specific state DOT planning activities ranged from 13 to 24 percent (see figure 14). RPOs most frequently reported dissatisfaction with state DOT activities related to determining the transportation priorities for rural areas of the state. Specific reasons RPOs cited for dissatisfaction vary, but include feeling that their needs are not prioritized, that there is a lack of support for rural planning, and that information gathered through consultation activities is not used to inform the statewide planning process.

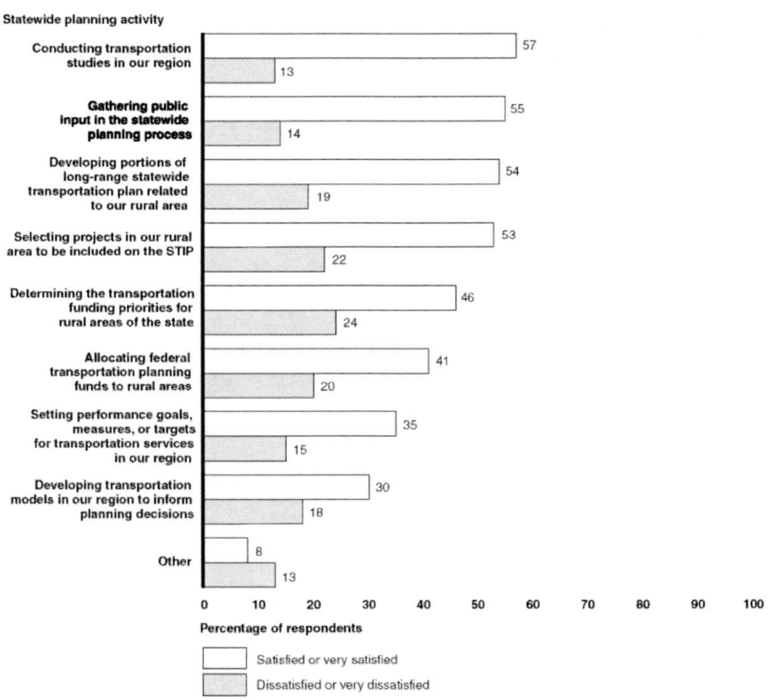

Source: Regional planning and development organization survey.

Figure 14. Surveyed RPOs' Satisfaction with Their Ability to Participate in State DOT Activities.

End Notes

[1] Funds deposited into the Highway Account of the Highway Trust Fund are primarily collected from taxes on motor fuels and truck-related items and distributed to the states using a series of formulas. States generally received more funding for highway programs than they contributed to the highway account of the trust fund in recent years because more funding was authorized and apportioned to states than was collected from the states and the account was supplemented by general funds from the U.S. Treasury. See GAO, *Highway Trust Fund: Nearly All States Received More Funding Than They Contributed in Highway Taxes Since 2005*, GAO-10-780 (Washington, D.C.: June 30, 2010).

[2] Pub. L. No. 111-147, Title IV, 124 Stat. 71, 78 (Mar. 18, 2010).

[3] GAO, *Surface Transportation: Restructured Federal Approach Needed for More Focused, Performance-Based, and Sustainable Programs*, GAO-08-400 (Washington, D.C.: Mar. 6, 2008).

[4] U.S. House of Representatives, Committee on Transportation and Infrastructure, *The Surface Transportation Authorization Act of 2009: A Blueprint for Investment and Reform* (Washington, D.C., June 18, 2009).

[5] Our discussion of state DOTs in this report includes the state DOTs in the 50 states as well as in the District of Columbia and Puerto Rico.

[6] States that employ such organizations refer to them by different names, including rural planning organizations, regional transportation planning organizations, and others. In this report, we use the general term RPO to refer to all such organizations.

[7] In some cases in this report we refer to the long-range statewide transportation plan as the long-range plan.

[8] 23 U.S.C. § 135(d) and 49 U.S.C. § 5304 (d).

[9] MPOs are required to review and update the metropolitan transportation plan at least every 4 years in air quality nonattainment and maintenance areas and at least every 5 years in attainment areas. An air quality nonattainment area is a region that the Environmental Protection Agency has designated as not meeting federal air quality standards. An air quality maintenance area is a region previously designated as a nonattainment area.

[10] 23 C.F.R. § 450.214(p).

[11] FHWA SPR funds are equal to 2 percent of each state's formula apportionment of funds for several programs, including the Congestion Mitigation and Air Quality Improvement, Equity Bonus, Highway Bridge, Highway Safety Improvement, National Highway System, Interstate Maintenance, and Surface Transportation programs. 23 U.S.C. § 505.

[12] FHWA is required to collect certain data to meet its responsibilities to Congress and the public, and it relies on states to collect some of these data through its HPMS. See 23 C.F.R. § 420.105(b). According to FHWA, HPMS data are also used for assessing highway system performance under FHWA's strategic planning process, including progress made toward meeting the objectives in FHWA's annual performance plan.

[13] In addition to statewide transportation planning funds, 1.25 percent of federal-aid highway funding from the Interstate Maintenance, National Highway System, Surface Transportation, Congestion Mitigation and Air Quality Improvement, and Highway Bridge programs is apportioned, based on population, to the states as metropolitan planning funds. Generally states then provide each of their MPOs with baseline funding and distribute any remaining balance according to a formula. See GAO, *Metropolitan Planning Organizations: Options Exist to Enhance Transportation Planning Capacity and Federal Oversight*, GAO-09-868 (Washington, D.C.: Sept. 9, 2009).

[14] According to federal statute, 17.28 percent of the amounts authorized for capital investment grants are allocated to FTA's SPRP for apportionment to each state according to a statutory formula. 49 U.S.C. § 5305 (g)(2).

[15] GAO-08-400.

[16] GAO-09-868.

[17] The measures proposed would address the degree to which the long-range metropolitan transportation plan reduces congestion, improves mobility and safety, and increases the state of good repair of surface transportation assets, among others. See Committee on Transportation and Infrastructure, *The Surface Transportation Authorization Act of 2009: A Blueprint for Investment and Reform.*

[18] GAO, *Federal-Aid Highways: FHWA Needs a Comprehensive Approach to Improving Project Oversight*, GAO-05-173 (Washington, D.C.: Jan. 31, 2005).

[19] GAO, *Highway Bridge Program: Condition of Nation's Bridges Shows Limited Improvement, but Further Actions Could Enhance the Impact of Federal Investment*, GAO-10-930T (Washington, D.C.: July 21, 2010).

[20] 23 C.F.R. § 450.214(b).

[21] GAO, *The Results Act: An Evaluator's Guide to Assessing Agency Annual Performance Plans*, GAO/GGD-10.1.20 (Washington, D.C.: April 1998).

[22] USDOT, FHWA, and FTA, *Statewide Opportunities for Integrating Operations, Safety, and Multimodal Planning: A Reference Manual,* FHWA-HEP-10-031 (Washington, D.C., May 2010).

[23] 23 U.S.C. § 135(d) and 49 U.S.C. § 5304(d).

[24] Pub. L. No. 103-62, 107 Stat. 285 (Aug. 3, 1993). GPRA requires federal agencies to set multiyear strategic goals in their strategic plans and corresponding annual goals in their performance plans, measure performance toward the achievement of those goals, and report on their progress in their annual performance reports.

[25] GAO/GGD-10.1.20.

[26] As discussed, 46 state DOTs reported inventorying the condition of existing transportation assets when developing their long-range statewide transportation plans.

[27] GAO-08-400.

[28] GAO, *Surface Transportation: Strategies Are Available for Making Existing Road Infrastructure Perform Better*, GAO-07-920 (Washington, D.C.: July 26, 2007).

[29] In general, an earmark is a congressional directive in legislation to a federal agency to spend a specific amount of its budget for a specific entity, project, or service. See GAO, Office of the General Counsel, *Principles of Federal Appropriations Law 3rd Edition*, vol. 2 (Washington, D.C.: February 2006).

[30] USDOT, Office of Inspector General, *Review of Congressional Earmarks within Department of Transportation Programs* (Washington, D.C., Sept. 7, 2007).

[31] FHWA division offices and FTA regional offices administer and obligate funds for projects to grant recipients and respond to questions from recipients on issues related to eligibility and transferability, among other things.

[32] GAO, *Congressional Directives: Selected Agencies' Processes for Responding to Funding Instructions,* GAO-08-209 (Washington, D.C.: Jan. 31, 2008)

[33] The economic analyses referred to in our survey were (1) benefit-cost analysis, used to identify the alternative with the greatest net benefit by comparing the monetary value of benefits and costs of each alternative; (2) cost-effectiveness analysis, used to identify the lowest cost alternative for achieving a level of benefit by comparing the costs of each alternative; and (3) economic impact analysis, used to identify the impact of alternatives on the local, regional, or national economy by measuring the effects derived from each alternative.

[34] USDOT, FHWA, Office of Asset Management, *Economic Analysis Primer* (Washington, D.C., August 2003).

[35] GAO, *Highway and Transit Investments: Options for Improving Information on Projects' Benefits and Costs and Increasing Accountability for Results*, GAO-05-172 (Washington, D.C.: Jan. 24, 2005).

[36] Pub. L. No. 111-5, Division A, Title XII, 123 Stat. 115, 203 (Feb. 17, 2009).

[37] See appendix I for the process that we used to identify planning challenges.

[38] For example, the Transportation Equity Act for the 21st Century's authorization of $171 billion for the Federal-Aid Highway Program from fiscal years 1998 through 2003 represented an increase of 41 percent over the $121 billion authorized in the prior 6-year bill. See GAO, *Federal-Aid Highways: Trends, Effect on State Spending, and Options for Future Program Design,* GAO-04-802 (Washington, D.C.: Aug. 31, 2004).

[39] GAO-04-802.

[40] Insufficient funds was the most frequently cited STIP development challenge. It was also the third most frequently cited long-range planning challenge, after involving the public, which was identified by 20 state DOTs, and data limitations, identified by 18 state DOTs.

[41] For some FHWA and FTA programs, for example, FHWA's Surface Transportation Program, and Congestion Mitigation and Air Quality Improvement Program, and FTA's Urbanized Area Formula Grants, funding for eligible activities may be used for either highway or transit programs. For these programs, states may transfer, or flex, certain funding among some programs, and between FHWA and FTA.

[42] See 23 C.F.R. § 450.104 and 23 C.F.R § 450.216(n).

[43] Administrative modifications to the STIP do not have these requirements and are therefore less burdensome administratively.

[44] 23 C.F.R. § 450.214(p).

[45] Through the enactment of SAFETEA-LU in August 2005, Congress statutorily established time frames for updating metropolitan transportation plans. MPOs are required to review and update the metropolitan transportation plan at least every 4 years in air quality nonattainment and maintenance areas and at least every 5 years in attainment areas.

[46] One state DOT did not indicate whether it had issued more than one long-range plan.

[47] 23 C.F.R. § 420.111 and § 420.115.

[48] Individual averages ranged from $2.9 million to $50.1 million per year.

[49] For instance, SAFETEA-LU added a requirement that the long-range statewide transportation plan include a discussion of potential environmental mitigation activities, to be developed in consultation with federal, state, and tribal wildlife, land management, and regulatory agencies.

[50] Those programs were Projects of National and Regional Significance, the National Corridor Infrastructure Improvement Program, and Coordinated Border Infrastructure.

[51] Pub. L. No. 109-59, Title III, § 3006(b) and Title VI, §6001(b) provide that "The Secretary shall not require a State or metropolitan planning organization to deviate from its established planning update cycle to implement changes made by this section. Beginning July 1, 2007, State or metropolitan planning organization plan or program updates shall reflect changes made by this section."

[52] GAO, *Rail Transit: Additional Federal Leadership Would Enhance FTA's State Safety Oversight Program*, GAO-06-821 (Washington, D.C.: July 26, 2006) and GAO-08-400.

[53] USDOT officials generally agreed with our recommendations and stated that, although they do have some performance measures in place for certain programs, additional performance measures could be beneficial.

[54] 23 U.S.C. § 133(d)(4),(e)(1).

[55] Conditional approval indicates that FHWA and FTA have determined that corrective actions need to be taken before the STIP can be found to meet or substantially meet federal planning requirements. Partial approval indicates that FHWA and FTA have approved the STIP for only a specific geographic area of a state.

[56] SAFETEA-LU required all states to develop a statewide-coordinated, strategic highway safety plan that provides a comprehensive framework for reducing highway fatalities and serious injuries on all public roads. The plan is to strategically establish statewide goals, objectives, and key emphasis areas developed in consultation with federal, state, local, and private sector safety stakeholders. States are also required to establish an evaluation process to analyze and assess results achieved by highway safety improvement projects. See 23 U.S.C. § 148.

[57] As noted previously, states are required to collect certain data on the condition of public roads, including pavement condition data, and report periodically to FHWA's HPMS program. Similarly, states must inspect and report on the condition of their bridges, generally every 2 years, through FHWA's National Bridge Inspection Program.

[58] USDOT recently published guidance on applying livability measures. See USDOT, *Livability in Transportation Guidebook: Planning Approaches That Promote Livability*, FHWA-HEP-10-028 (Washington, D.C., September 2010).

[59] See, for example, GAO, *Executive Guide: Effectively Implementing the Government Performance and Results Act,* GAO/GGD-96-118 (Washington, D.C.: June 1996) and GAO-08-400.

[60] USDOT, International Technology Scanning Program, *Linking Transportation Performance and Accountability,* FHWA-PL-10-011, (Washington, D.C., April 2010). This international scan study was sponsored by FHWA, the American Association of State Highway and Transportation Officials, and the National Cooperative Highway Research Program. The report focused on the experiences of Australia, Great Britain, New Zealand, and Sweden.

[61] GAO-08-400.

[62] GAO/GGD-96-118.

[63] For example, see USDOT, *Traffic Safety Performance Measures for States and Federal Agencies*, DOT HS 811 025 (Washington, D.C., August 2008).

[64] Office of Management and Budget, Circular No. A-11.

[65] GAO, *Results-Oriented Management: Strengthening Key Practices at FEMA and Interior Could Promote Greater Use of Performance Information,* GAO-09-676 (Washington, D.C.: Aug. 17, 2009).

[66] GAO, *Managing for Results: Enhancing Agency Use of Performance Information for Management Decision Making,* GAO-05-927 (Washington, D.C.: Sept. 9, 2005).

[67] Federal provisions for statewide transportation planning are in 23 U.S.C. § 135 and 49 U.S.C. § 5304. Federal Highway Administration and Federal Transit Administration regulations implementing these provisions are in 23 C.F.R. part 450, subpart B.

[68] States that employ such organizations refer to them by different names, including rural planning organizations, regional transportation planning organizations, and others. In this report, we use the general term RPO to refer to all such organizations.

[69] Through our survey of regional planning and development organizations, we asked survey respondents to indicate whether they coordinate or conduct surface transportation or transit planning in nonmetropolitan areas. For the purposes of this report, we refer to organizations that perform such activities as RPOs. Survey responses from organizations reporting that they did not coordinate or conduct surface transportation or transit planning in nonmetropolitan areas are not included in this appendix. The complete results of this survey are available in GAO-11-78SP. For information on our survey methodology, see appendix I.

INDEX

D

E

F

P

Q

R

S

T

U

V

W